THEHUMANSEARCHENGINE

It's what you *think* you know about a job search that keeps you unemployed.

CHRIS CZARNIK | CHRISTOPHER JOSSART

© 2013 Chris Czarnik and Christopher Jossart

All rights reserved. No part of this publication may be reproduced or transmitted in any form or by any means, electronic, hard copy, or mechanical, including photocopying and recording, or by any information storage and retrieval system without written permission from the authors.

ISBN: 978-0-615-74813-9

The Myths of a job search are:

Number one, open jobs are always advertised and filled through HR.

Number two, job search is random and based on luck.

Number three, job search is out of my control.

The Truth is:

Old job search methods are the problem.

Human Search Engine is the solution.

Dedication~

There are certain people and organizations that have touched my life. Without these important people and places, my work in teaching job search would not be possible, nor would this book.

Dr. Susan May, president of Fox Valley Technical College, Appleton, Wisconsin, and Bruce Weiland, director of Student Employment Services at Fox Valley Technical College. To both of you, thanks for believing in me and for seeing my potential before I did. I am forever grateful.

Caroline Lasecki, my friend and confidant. She brought me in as a career search client and then became a co-worker at the national career search firm where I learned the building blocks of job search. You kept me going when I doubted that this was the right path for me.

Jamie Voster, my friend and colleague at Fox Valley Technical College. She supported two years-worth of my presentations and tutored students on job search methods. I treasure every challenge you presented me with to make this understandable and useable for everyone.

Chris Jossart, co-author of this book and a true partner of the process. He presented the book idea to me after he learned about the process while helping promote it at Fox Valley Technical College. Thanks, Chris, for your support and editorial direction in seeing this through.

Chris and I collectively want to extend a huge thanks to the many displaced workers who trusted us with the job search over the past five years in this new economy. They have inspired us with a can-do attitude and their desire to take control of their lives. We are forever proud of your accomplishments.

My children Andrea, Scott, and Ben. I am so much a better man because of your unyielding belief in me. You have been the greatest gifts in my life and a daily source of pride . Scott, our conversation on the way to the train station was a pivotal moment for me. thank you.

And finally and most importantly to the love of my life and greatest supporter, my wife Carlene. Your encouragement to follow this dream when it was only a dream has changed my life and the lives of so many others. You are the best thing that has ever happened to me.

—*Chris Czarnik*

Contents~

Prologue~ 1

Preface~ 5

Chapter 1 7
    A new way to succeed in a new economy
    This is no infomercial; it's about finding anything of value in your life

Chapter 2 11
    I don't know you, but here is $4,000
    My failed 'Hail Mary' pass at job search

Chapter 3 15
    A Sheep in a Wolf's Den
    I now worked for the company that deceived me!

Chapter 4 19
    Everyday guy brings a job secret to the streets
    I better arrive early to teach this stuff!

Chapter 5 23
    The envelope, please. Your ideal job starts with a blank page.
    Why go back to what you had?

Chapter 6 27
    Precursor 1 to the Process:
        Expect the unexpected, but expect results:
        How your HSE Search will likely go.

Chapter 7 31
    Precursor 2 to the Process:
        Be humble, be sincere, ask for help.

Chapter 8 35
    Precursor 3 to the Process:
        No one knows you exist, and you are unaware of at least 85% of
        companies that would hire you right now.

Chapter 9 37
    Precursor 4 to the Process:
        Get to know YOU. You won't need to change yourself
        for anyone or for any job.

Chapter 10 39
    Instructional Unit Preface

Chapter 11 43
    DEFINING
    What to do at 8:00 a.m. each morning.
      A step-by-step guide to the new job search process.
    The *Human Search Engine* INSTRUCTIONAL PROCESS STEP 1:

Chapter 12 49
    DEFINING
    The *Human Search Engine* INSTRUCTIONAL PROCESS STEP 2:

Chapter 13 53
    DEFINING
    The *Human Search Engine* INSTRUCTIONAL PROCESS STEP 3:

Chapter 14 57
    UNIT RECAP: Definition

Chapter 15 59
    RESEARCH
    The *Human Search Engine* INSTRUCTIONAL PROCESS STEP 4:

Chapter 16 67
    RESEARCH
    The *Human Search Engine* INSTRUCTIONAL PROCESS STEP 5:

Chapter 17 73
    UNIT RECAP: Research

Chapter 18 75
    MARKETING (YOU)
    The *Human Search Engine* INSTRUCTIONAL PROCESS STEP 6:

Chapter 19 85
    MARKETING (YOU)
    The *Human Search Engine* INSTRUCTIONAL PROCESS STEP 7:

Chapter 20 97
    MARKETING (YOU)
    The *Human Search Engine* INSTRUCTIONAL PROCESS STEP 8:

Chapter 21 103
    MARKETING (YOU)
    The *Human Search Engine* INSTRUCTIONAL PROCESS STEP 9:

Chapter 22 109
    MARKETING (YOU)
    The *Human Search Engine* INSTRUCTIONAL PROCESS STEP 10:

Chapter 23 119
    MARKETING (YOU)
    The *Human Search Engine* INSTRUCTIONAL PROCESS STEP 11:

Chapter 24 123
    UNIT RECAP: Marketing

Chapter 25 127
    HITTING THE STREETS

Chapter 26 131
    HITTING THE STREETS

Chapter 27 141
    A Plumber's Journey:
        Your *Human Search Engine* model landing story.

Chapter 28 145
    Landings! Real People, Real Careers through *HSE*
    Think differently. You are different
    You can't push your way into a job. I was pulled in.
    I Thought I Knew Everything About Searching for a Job. Ouch.
    Career Planners and Job Fairs: Why was I Still Unemployed?

Chapter 29 155
    Employers: Welcome to Smart Hiring
    Smart companies don't make half-a-million-dollar decisions off of a piece of paper

Inquiries: 163

About The Authors: 164

Acknowledgements 167

Prologue~

Jobseekers are desperate to take control of their job search, but how can they with unemployment rates and recession talks dominating the news and political scene like never before? Ironically, even in stable economies, jobseekers have never really had control of their job search. What gives?

Until now, all career search advice books basically convey the same approach. These publications all outline vague generalities that leave a jobseeker curious, but they by no means teach a step-by-step process. *Human Search Engine (HSE)* is that process reimagined and revised from the grips of corporate greed. It is designed to give jobseekers a plan each morning to make something happen for themselves.

Enter Chris Czarnik—the "Czar of Career Search Strategy." His method of teaching job search both as a skill and as a controllable process (using a project management methodology) has been successful for more than 10 years. He has coached hundreds of individuals through one-on-one consultation and thousands of people by way of workshops and speaking engagements. As a career counselor, he has written job search curriculum for several colleges, including the fifth largest research university in the nation. He speaks to thousands of students and jobseekers every year about controlling their own destiny.

Through *HSE,* the Czar teaches you how to tap into a hiring process that at one time was only available to the fortunate few who could pay thousands of dollars. More importantly, his process is based on clear and easy-to-understand steps that you can start on the moment you delve into this book.

HSE changes the job search game in your favor and bypasses the endless black hole of sending resumes and cover letters with no replies. Control over your job search is both a navigable and rewarding process. and here are the keys to start the engine on behalf of the *Czar.* He shared his story with me about 'Steve' to demonstrate the power of the process.

Steve's Story: From Shawano, Wisconsin to the White House

After more than a decade of teaching career search, I have met many amazing people and seen incredible transformations from individuals who embrace the *Human Search Engine* process. These success stories often boggle the mind. While writing this book, I smiled at myself because as I have told others, "The stories are so incredible that I'm going to need to publish it under fiction." Among all of these compelling stories, one sticks out more than the rest. the story of Steve Golubic.

THE HUMAN SEARCH ENGINE

I first met Steve as a client after I had taught career search for a couple of years. He came to our initial meeting uncertain and afraid. While that is not entirely unusual for job search clients, there was something different here—I recognized him.

Steve had spent the majority of his working life in the emergency management field, and he was good at it. His work was all about preparing for and responding to emergency situations like tornados, floods, mass chemical spills, and other natural and man-made disasters. His job was one that you and I spend very little time thinking about—until we need it.

One area of his expertise was in managing the situation and resources that come into play immediately after a disaster strikes. His ability to prepare for disasters that had not yet occurred was as equally important, but he was the person in the headlines when an incident occurred. If you have ever thought, "Wow, somebody should do something about that horrible disaster," then Steve was the person you were referring to.

I recognized his name from some seven or eight years earlier. There had been a train derailment near Weyauwega, a small city in east central Wisconsin. The train cars that derailed were filled with toxic chemicals. It was all over the news, and citizens of Weyauwega and surrounding communities had to completely evacuate the area as it was quarantined for a massive clean-up effort.

Steve was a member of the Incident Commander Team regarding the response to this tragedy. He was recognized later as having done an incredible job organizing and executing the response and recovery efforts as part of the team. His work on behalf of hundreds of other responders was acknowledged across the state.

The subsequent years after this incident had not been kind to Steve's career. Through a series of budget cuts and a de-emphasizing of emergency management at various government levels, his position had been reduced over and over again. When Steve finally walked into my office he was barely hanging onto a 20 hour-a-week job in the smaller community of Shawano, Wisconsin. Even worse, that position was in danger of being reduced even further and perhaps eliminated altogether. The term Steve used in our first meeting was that he had gone from the "penthouse to the outhouse." He was scared, humbled, and lost in his search.

As with every other client, I simply started to walk him through my process (That's what is cool about *HSE* being a process. Whether the client is an astronaut or a circus clown, the process remains the same. Whatever your area of expertise is in, the process is the answer. and that's why it can work for anyone.). We walked through achievements and skills, objectives, and Networking Briefs. Through the process I could see that Steve's confidence was returning. He began to realize that his skills and abilities hadn't changed; it was just that the right people weren't seeing him that way at the moment.

We started our search by identifying people who had been critical to Steve's success with the emergency management work he did so successfully in the past (his ABC List). Then we determined that his work with a few of the local Native American tribes turned out to be some of his most successful and enjoyable endeavors. He made a list of people who he had conversed with during these tribal experiences. It was comprised of contacts that had a high level of confidence in him. He proceeded to set up Networking Meetings and Informational Interviews with them.

To Steve's great surprise, these people were very WILLING to help him with his search because they remembered him for the great work he had done for them in the past. While his opinion of himself had faded, these people treated him as an invaluable resource. In a short period of time (two or maybe three connections later), he was asked to do some part-time emergency planning for one of the local tribes. He was thrilled! Someone thought he was good enough again!

Now convinced in the power of the process, Steve didn't stop. During his part-time work he was coming into contact with dozens of people who lived in the world of emergency management. He was making strong connections and building relationships. His Informational Interviews with these people centered on where his skill set might be most valued. It wasn't long before his reputation spread throughout the Native American community. Eventually a number of tribes created a full-time position through a Federal grant. That's right. a position that was never advertised was born through the process. He wasn't done yet in making this story even more astonishing.

Steve continued to network (the right way as taught by the process) in the emergency management sector not knowing he would need it again. Once again he found himself facing the same dilemma. The new position was being eliminated and Steve would be jobless in a few months. He took action this time by using the network he built and immediately sent notifications to people within this circle of diverse individuals.

It was not long before one of his connections asked Steve if he would like to come and work for FEMA (Federal Emergency Management Agency) to help with the flooding from hurricane Katrina in New Orleans. Steve jumped at the opportunity. from part-time in Shawano to a full-time contractor with FEMA in less than a year and a half, but that's not where the story ends.

I am proud to say that through a series of promotions, Steve became a manager in the FEMA organization and was transferred to Washington D.C. After about five years of diligent work, he has become one of the go-to-individuals in Washington in his area of expertise, and within the past year (2011–12), he was named the Director of Tribal Affairs for the Department of Homeland Security. That's right. the same guy who was seen by others as barely good enough to hang onto a part-time job in a town of 10,000 in east central Wisconsin now attends briefings in the White House. Not bad, huh?

I met with Steve while writing this book to ask his permission to put his story in it. Amazingly (or maybe not so), he was the exact same humble guy that I had met years earlier. In fact, that's one of the secrets to his success. **Be humble, be sincere, and ask for help.** I want you to remember these three concepts throughout this entire book! Over lunch with our families in a crab shack in Annapolis, Maryland, he gave his consent to be in the book. With a smile he said, "Go ahead and put me in the book, but nobody's ever going to believe it."

As I mentioned earlier in Steve's story, I think I'm going to have to publish this under fiction.

Preface~

The reason for this book is that jobseekers and employers can't find each other.

One day after teaching my job search class at the college, I was scheduled to deliver a short address to 15 HR people and hiring managers from mid- to large-size companies. My presentation was intended to be a very small part of a bigger conversation about the college's overall services to the community.

Initially, I sat at one of the tables and greeted attendees from some of these businesses and introduced myself to them. Some of the guests had vaguely heard about the job search program I was teaching at the college. Whatever small talk that was occurring elsewhere at the table immediately ceased. People at the table quickly became involved in the topic of searching for talented new employees.

"Where is all the talent out there, Chris?" asked one of the HR persons. The faces of almost all of the company reps at my table turned to me with looks of frustration. The same person continued, "We have been advertising for an operations manager with specific skills for nearly three months now, and the resumes we have received don't fit at all. It's like the applicants aren't reading the ad and just applying using generic resumes and cover letters, regardless of if they actually are qualified to do the job," he concluded.

There was implied agreement from at least half of the company reps at the table that this appeared to be a real problem for them as well. I wanted to stand on my chair and yell, "The talented people who you are looking for are just down the hall in my job search class!" I usually jump at these opportunities to provide helpful information, but I didn't. I was so taken by what I just heard that I froze.

A few minutes later 'something' hit me: **The biggest problem in job search is that employers and jobseekers can't find each other.**

A 'new economy' has ushered new challenges. Day after day, year after year, we follow a failing system in the process of hiring. Consequently, this level of failure not only impacts our quality of life as individuals, but it negates economic growth.

Here is a plan I can offer as a current ripple that is growing into a small wave of real success. Since 2009, many people have called me the "Czar of Career Search Strategy." Although humbling, it is certainly life-changing for me to reflect on the impact of empowering hundreds of jobseekers land rewarding careers. I ask myself how something that appears so simple could take so long to come to light.

HSE presents a step-by-step "here's what you can do each day at 8:00 a.m. approach" to changing your life, professionally and even personally. It is a no-frills, curriculum-based process that is quantifiably working (in just three years, *HSE* has helped land meaningful jobs for hundreds of people). This book will introduce to you a small sample of real people who have landed their next career through *HSE*. I only wish I could share all of their stories with you! They are happening every week where I teach this process at Fox Valley Technical College in Appleton, Wisconsin under the name, JobSeekers Network.[1]

These new beginnings for jobseekers do not represent ho-hum careers either. Most *HSE* job landings make a person want to get out of bed in the morning to take on the challenges of the day. That's what makes this process innovative. It is **logical**, **sequential**, **experiential**, and **terminal**.

There are two signs that hang in my office in Appleton. One of them is a psychology quote, "If you always do what you've always done, you'll always get what you always got." The message is clear—if something is not working, then find another way. The other sign displays the words of the late (great) Steven Covey, "Seek first to understand—then to be understood." These words signify *HSE* to the core. In your job search, stop talking and start listening; the path will be made clear to you. These two phrases will guide your *HSE* journey.

My promise to you as creator of the *HSE* process is this: No infomercial quick fix remedies. just a logical step-by-step process that you control. Do the work, commit to the process, and your efforts will define your results. isn't that all you are asking for?"

Chapter 1

A new way to succeed in a new economy

This is no infomercial; it's about finding anything of value in your life

I love playing darts, but I don't see dart boards in every home I visit. I'm surprised. I thought that consumers find the best homebuilders (or anything else) by throwing darts at the wall. Sarcasm aside at least just for now let me ask you, "Why would you find your next job the same way?" Maybe instead of resumes and cover letters, we ought to be looking at dart boards for guidance in our next job!

The reality is that like throwing darts, the majority of jobseekers believe that random saturation is the way to land their next career. *It's what you THINK you know about job search that keeps you UNEMPLOYED.* Less than 25% of all jobs are filled through job placement agencies, by attending job fairs, and through classified advertising on the Web or in newspapers, according to my 11 years in the field and related research.

What about the remaining 75% of jobs? How are they filled? The answer is through people or networking, but not just any networking. The difference with the *Human Search Engine (HSE)* brand of networking is that the process is logical, sequential, experiential, and terminal. There is strategy and manageability behind this plan, and it is faster than conventional job search.

Conventional job search methods like newspaper ads, staffing agency listings, and other advertising-related tactics that once worked regularly have now hit a brick wall. They don't work as well today. In addition, jobs are going overseas and high unemployment rates are molding into societal norms. It's time to adjust.

Jobseekers are inundating this economy. The vast wave of layoffs that grabbed the United States workforce in 2008 has created an alarming sense of urgency and uncertainty among Americans. On the other hand, the American economy is suffering from a major skills gap. If addressed proactively, this is a good problem that lies before us. There are rewarding careers for people with the right skills.

For example, as of late summer 2012, there were more than 1,700 full-time jobs for skilled professionals in a five-county region in northeast Wisconsin. The repository-based listing of these jobs is made available regularly by a two-year community college for its students. 2

At the same time, the national media aren't doing anything to help spur confidence. Go figure. Members of the media represent powerful voices and are accountable to no one, and they make a grass-roots resurgence like the *Human Search Engine* tough to spread the word about because it is positive and self-empowering. Since the economic crash of 2008, all that has been told about the job outlook by the media is doom and gloom. Good news doesn't sell. Once awareness spreads about this process, I am crossing my fingers that mass media will jump on some good news half as aggressively as they do bad news. The *HSE* process is all about self-empowerment and a better quality of life.

Admittedly, the economic state of the nation is unhealthy, but we have done little to adjust to what this new economy needs. Rather, the sluggish economy has only fueled political blame. There's only one way to combat these destructive and powerful influences if you are out of work or unhappy with your current employment. You must take control of your next career. It is a tough time for your neighbor who lost his job at a paper company after 30 years, or for your friend who has been displaced from her retail management position after 12 years. Maybe it is a difficult time for you, too?

As history suggests, the current economy could really be just a big hiccup. Our nation (and world) has witnessed roller coaster economies before—what's different now? Without detailing issues surrounding over-population, unprecedented natural disasters and world crises, continuous political gridlock, and increased global competition, can we admit just once that our society doesn't do a good job of adjusting to hiccups in changing economies? After all, it's now been over four years with this so-called recession and not much has changed.

Maybe the way we do business and the methods in which we train the next generation workforce no longer work like they did in the 20th century. Maybe we have ushered in a 'new economy' that has finally hit us between the eyes because we failed to prepare for the future. Regardless of whether you argue that we're in a recession or in a 'new economy,' the time to absorb a fresh way of thinking is now.

As noted earlier, good-paying jobs for *skilled workers* (yes, let's all agree that assembly-line jobs for high school graduates that pay $18 an hour are basically gone) are available. Hiring managers are desperate to find talent, but the current way companies find quality employees is expensive, long, and risky in terms of obtaining a good match that fits the position technically and dynamically.

Before thinking you can jump aboard a magic trolley to a land where a laundry list of great jobs will appear, you must stoke the **process** known as the *Human Search Engine (HSE)*. The answer regarding your next career and maybe your last is in this **process**. WARNING: As I tell my jobseekers and students, this process is designed to kick you in the butt (so learn to take a little humility and absorb a fresh outlook along the way).

Chapter 2

I don't know you, but here is $4,000

My failed 'Hail Mary' pass at job search

In February of 2002, I became extremely unhappy with my job as the operations manager for a small paper converting company in northeast Wisconsin. I was desperately looking for a way out of that job. The new president of the company had been replaced by a person, who in my opinion, was willing to put profit before people. I was hoping to give the new president a chance, but my instinct suggested otherwise.

The president came to the company at a time when it was badly struggling. The paper converting part of the organization had started at the wrong time. About the time when the new equipment arrived and we had been through a big machine start-up process, the paper industry collapsed. The expansion concept for the company was good; the timing was terrible.

The original president was replaced by someone who had been called a "turn around boss." For those who haven't been exposed to this concept, "turn around boss" is also often referred to as "the hatchet boss." This person's job is to do whatever it takes to restore a company's profitability and stability, regardless of the effects the changes have on people. In my years in business, these actions usually involved quick layoffs, drastic cost-cutting measures, threatening people with their jobs, unrealistic demands, and a great deal of emotional pain and added stress in the organization.

From the first day under the leadership of the new president, it became clear to me that he was capable of virtually anything. My most notable memories involve this little man standing in the middle of the office screaming at people in an effort to "motivate" them. Three-hour staff meetings on Monday mornings were the norm. They consisted of mostly our new leader screaming about how incompetent we all were and how he would be so much better off if he just replaced us all and started over. In one particularly painful meeting, the president went so far as to threaten all of us with closing the plant. At wits end, I stood up and said, "That's no threat. If you close this place, my life gets **better**!"

(By the way, while writing this book, this SAME person some 10 years later inquired about the process I teach because he was in need of a new job! I still can't believe it!)

It was clear my time with that organization was short. I had to find another job, but I was scared and beaten down. I also now realized that I never really wanted to be in the paper industry or manufacturing. For the first time in my life, I really wanted to examine it, along with my skills and what job would be a great fit for me. But how?

Coming to Haldane

During my time at the paper converting company, my wife begged me to leave that job. She knew long before I did that I was not cut out to be in manufacturing, even though I had done well in the field, earning several promotions. Deep down I knew she was right, but I was far too afraid and denigrated to even begin to make a switch on my own. The money was good, but the job was terrible. I found myself in "golden handcuffs."

Then, in the Sunday newspaper I saw an ad posted by Bernard Haldane & Associates. I can't recall exactly what the ad said, but to me I saw a way out. It appeared to be a recruiting firm for management professionals. The ad seemed to infer opportunities for new management positions. It was very encouraging, and I called to set up a meeting with the company. That call turned out to be the best, and the worst call I ever made.

> *"That's the funny thing about being unemployed; it turns smart resourceful people into beggars with a cup in their hand looking for a miracle."*

As I look back, it was silly of me not to do any research on the organization that I was going to meet with despite a lack of resources compared to today. The Internet was in its early stages, and there was no such thing as a "Google" search, or if it was around, the search engine culture was certainly not a common practice like it is today. I was in a desperate spot and seeking a miracle. I guess I saw what I wanted to see. That's the funny thing about being unemployed; it turns smart resourceful people into beggars with a cup in their hand looking for a miracle. As I soon discovered, Haldane was readily poised to take advantage of desperate jobseekers, yes, just like me.

At Haldane, I met with a young vibrant representative during my first meeting. She seemed incredibly confident and was very articulate. It was much later that I learned she was following a very structured script—one so persuasive that it would give presidential script writers a run for their money. These well-crafted scripts were used in Haldane's offices around the country. She spoke of opportunity, finding my real value, and finding a perfect fit for a place to work. It sounded too good to be true. and you know what's "said" about things that seem too good to be true—they usually are.

The second meeting required the presence of my wife. Again, looking back, that should have been a signal. Really, we know how to truly make a sale stick, right? The spouse needs sign off on the deal as well! The same young woman talked us through the idea that Haldane was the path to happiness and work fulfillment. It was only when she presented us with a contract that my jaw dropped!

The contract fee was $4,250.00! There was NO WAY I was going to proceed. My wife, however, saw it as an opportunity to help me find a place where I could be happy again. With tears in our eyes, we put the fee on a credit card and signed the contract.

No Light in this Tunnel

I tried with all the faith I had to embark on finding one of these "hidden" jobs Haldane had been advertising. I realistically felt, however, I would have a better chance of finding the Holy Grail before I would a job—and even *any* job at this point. Even then, I was starting to believe it was going to take a Hail Mary pass to land anything. I got myself in deep in something so uncertain. There was no light in this tunnel.

The next step brought a little relief. Surprisingly, and much-needed in terms of my confidence, I was assigned to what appeared to be a fine man of business who had a good heart and strong constitution. Our meetings, however, didn't discuss those "hidden" job opportunities that I heard about (reflecting back, I now realize that was all a sales pitch). We worked on achievements and personality types, but where were the great jobs and interviews that had been alluded to in the initial meetings?

I inquisitively addressed the "hidden job" component of my career-planning investment with the advisor during our second meeting. He explained to me that there really was no list of "hidden" jobs that Haldane had access to. He was going to teach me a process that was going to allow me to search for those hidden opportunities. I was incensed. I felt stupid and used and I let him know it!

I could tell my advisor had engaged in the same discussion before. I imagined how many people he had disclosed this same "tweak of the truth" to every week. This appeared to me to be a clear case of bait and switch: *promise jobs and deliver training*. I was now incredibly upset that I had spent more money on this misleading service than most people spent on a used car.

The culmination of my training was a market campaign seminar on a Saturday morning. I, along with four other clients, sat through a three-hour presentation on how to hold "informational interviews" in order to conduct our search using the process. I left that meeting again fuming, "This is what I get for $4,250?!" I wasn't sure what I was going to do with the information; I felt deflated and hopeless.

I had left the converting company about a month after starting the Haldane program because I was pumped up with confidence that this contract I signed would positively change my life. Now I was unemployed, had no job leads or a career game plan, and was out $4,250.

Chapter 3

A Sheep in a Wolf's Den

I now worked for the company that deceived me!

In the weeks that followed the market campaign seminar at Haldane, I felt bad about my decision to go with the firm in the first place, but I was also very interested in its process. I kept thinking the process had merit, but the way it was taught did not make me at all prepared to actually do that type of search. I was also still reeling from the unethical bait and switch marketing ploys that lured me into that difficult and distrustful experience.

Fate seems to have a sense of humor. About three weeks after my training ended, I was informed that my Haldane advisor was retiring and that his spot was open. My advisor had thought of me as a possible replacement based on my communication skills and understanding of the process. After two interviews I was hired as the new advisor at Haldane. That's right. I went to work for the very organization that I felt had misled me. Call it desperation, call it believing that there was a better way to do the training, but I was now "the sheep in a wolf's den."

Again, the original purpose of Haldane's career search process was well-intended—starting as a result of helping military veterans at the end of World War II. The gentleman himself, Bernard Haldane, championed a life-changing movement known as the Dependable Strengths Articulation Process (DSAP).[3] He literally empowered thousands of people over the years through his ingenious vision. For a long time the company was well-respected, honest, and effective. For about the next 25 years, if you received outplacement or career counseling from a Haldane office, it was the best you could get!

As Haldane aged, he decided to sell the business in 1974. Haldane offices were sold as franchises and sprung up across the country. The seeds that would end in charges by multiple Attorneys General had been planted.

Walking the Line

The following is part of a string of e-mail exchanges dated April 1, 2004 that occurred while I was employed at Bernard Haldane & Associates. The string of correspondence (subject line—Leads/Sales) started by a member of the organization's leadership team to two sales associates (who also served as preliminary advisors to clients). The email was then forwarded to me later that same day as an "FYI." The names involved in this correspondence are both anonymous and fictitious.

> *[leadership member]* I would like to encourage you guys to get together and review your pre-lim and call-back process. You finished the month dead last (in revenue). One last question, "Are you walking close enough to the line?" [4]
>
> *[sales associate's response]* I don't think I have been walking close enough to the line. I think my fear of Jake (another sales rep not included in the e-mail) "setting things straight" in the first meeting (with a client) caused a refund. Make sense? [4]
>
> *[leadership member's response]* Who was it that wanted us to hire Jake? Either you set him straight that you have to walk the line in order to bring on clients for all of us to exist, or I will, that came straight from Kurt (another leader) as well. We got into this in Appleton with Chris Czarnik. Simply put, if he cannot deliver what you promise, someone else can be trained to do so. [4]

The e-mail exchange didn't end there, but as you can see, Haldane's leadership centered on "walking a thin line" between honesty and expectations. Sales associates were required to stretch expectations just enough to make clients excitedly sign the bottom line for their next dream job, while at the same time, preventing the issuance of refunds. Client contention for refunds stemmed from being presented unrealistic expectations, in which I lived as a client and now as an advisor trying to change an unhealthy practice.

That same e-mail exchange ended with the leader saying, *If we don't walk close to the line, we would not get new clients,* and a thought-provoking ending. *Is your armor plate wearing thin?* To me, the culture of that Haldane office at the time exuded a 'whatever-it-takes to sell for profit attitude' with little or no regard for people.

As a new advisor, I took great pains to explain to clients what the process "was and was not." Once clients understood it was a process in which they had complete control over and that it would better their lives in other areas too, this pioneering job search method kicked into overdrive in my mind. I employed supplemental tactics to help clients land jobs. My first client landed and exuberantly shouted, "AWESOME! IT WORKS!"

Over the next year there were dozens of happy clients and numerous letters of recommendation. If people were willing to do the work, they succeeded! I was also very up front with people about what would be required of them during this process. I told them that if they didn't do the work, their job search would fail. I could swallow this approach of open disclosure because it was ethical.

Our clients were landing jobs even as rumblings of lawsuits against other Haldane offices (which were owned by franchisees) surfaced for misrepresentation. The peak of that ironic juxtaposition hit us front and center in 2002. We were at a training in Des Moines, Iowa when we heard on TV that a newscast was exposing what it called one of the biggest career search scams ever. Bernard Haldane & Associates.[5]

It was chilling to watch that program with others from the office. Here we had 30-plus letters of recommendation from my clients; many of them described their experience as the best money they had ever spent. At the same time, we were watching a national news broadcast showing undercover video from offices around the country (not ours) that seemed to clearly show misleading sales pitches delivered to desperate jobseekers. Suffice to say, we were flat out shocked!

I even had one past client who had written us a great letter of recommendation and had landed a really terrific job call and ask if he had been scammed by us. I asked him in a reassuring voice, "How did it work for you?" Although he was thrilled with his result, this was perhaps the lowest point in my entire career.

It was then I decided that teaching this life skill was too important to be tainted by this organization (which has since been successfully sued by a number of State Attorneys General). No one should have to write a check for $4,250 (and in some cases much more) to learn this basic life skill.

This process should be taught at least at the college level and maybe even during high school (especially in today's economy). We teach students to memorize the capitals of all 50 states, but we don't prepare them how to look for a job. how backwards is that? Everyone needs this; that's why I want to make it accessible for anyone from any walk of life as much as I can.

Chapter 4

Everyday guy brings a job secret to the streets

I better arrive early to teach this stuff!

"You're not going to believe who I talked to today!" declares a 50-plus year-old displaced worker to me at a free job search session that I currently teach three times a week in my post-Haldane world. Each session is well attended, anchored by steady regional media attention, a very active LinkedIn site, and yes of course, word-of-mouth advertising and networking. I am honored to partner with Fox Valley Technical College, the largest two-year college in Wisconsin (based on total number of people served), located in Appleton (about 35 miles south of the home of the Green Bay Packers).

The worker, who had lost his job after working 20 years in a supervisory position for a nearby manufacturer, had been attending my sessions for about four weeks. He wanted to learn what a friend had told him about a new way of looking for a job. After all, every method of looking for a job had failed him during the past year. newspapers, Web sites, workforce development seminars, etc.

The gentleman discloses to me whom he had talked to. It was no celebrity, no president promising hope and change, no reality television icon—this was all about making a connection in the workforce. What I've come to realize through teaching these job search sessions is that the real champions of jobseekers are real people like themselves. They are not people holding magic wands telling them there are hidden jobs somewhere. The result of this gentleman's disclosure was a barrage of spontaneous networking that occurred around the room by other jobseekers. This moment had a real impact on me. I had to do something about it.

After the session I quickly revised my 90-minute class—for good reason. I needed to allow more time for open-ended networking in-class to transpire. My simple revision on a blank piece of paper read: *I better arrive early to teach this stuff!* These types of informal discussions among jobseekers were an incredible validation to me that this newly crafted job search process was working! It was changing lives—one jobseeker at a time.

My sessions were starting to raise eyebrows throughout surrounding communities. Word was spreading fast, and the college's marketing and leadership teams supported the sessions with advertising and public relations activities to help them gain more visibility. I couldn't wait to get to work each morning. I started to check my email with excitement like it was Christmas morning as a kid. Why? The subject lines in my inbox increasingly read, "I did it!" or "I landed!"

Overwhelmingly humbled, my replies to these messages were filled with gratitude. I was thankful for being in a position to see good people find success in the form of a new career. Furthermore, their new career was one they were going to enjoy as well because jobseekers through the *Human Search Engine* (*HSE*) control the job search. No more **shots in the dark** at accepting a job based on putting your finger in the wind and hoping for a miracle. *HSE* removes that ill-fated equation that has been haunting jobseekers and companies for decades.

I wanted nothing in return from this humble recognition except a voice. I simply continue to ask these appreciative individuals to tell others that the ***process*** works so more people can improve their lives. I continue to receive "thank you" messages as more people attend the sessions. Once they attend, participants are part of an unabated network virtually immune to failure. The worst outcome they can encounter during the ***process*** is a fresh method toward solving any given problem. The best outcome is finding a rewarding career. Either way, the worst outcome really never occurs anyway because it is a precursor to the best outcome. If my jobseekers do the work and follow the process, they will succeed.

In just three-plus years, I have witnessed hundreds of jobseekers land careers by following a manageable, measurable process (the ones I actually know of—they aren't all reported on as people "move on"). I have documented testimonials from one of the fastest-growing LinkedIn groups around of people proclaiming that the *HSE* process works! More and more employers are looking into its benefits as a smart way to hire in today's arena of finding, developing, and retaining talent. The success of *HSE* has caught wildfire. More career development trainers and educational systems need to adopt the plan to meet the demands of our new economy and the dynamics of smart hiring companies.

What I teach has nothing to do with throwing your name and credentials across the fruited plain and seeing what kind of job you can land. I introduce a step-by-step process in which you know where you will land and with whom. *HSE* is not about the saturation of resumes in a world where HR professionals have less than seven seconds to know you on paper. Rather, my session will humble you in the first seven seconds of attending it. Humility will become your catalyst to learning a fresh skill that can be used basically for any part of life that is of value to you.

Finding value from a career perspective is not an easy task. Admittedly, I have learned from the best-of-the-best when it comes to reflecting on what's important in life, professionally speaking. In 2011, the process gave birth to a "50/50 Club."[6] Organic in its inception (I had nothing to do with it), this group represents individuals who are ages 50-plus with new jobs as a result of *HSE* making more than $50,000 a year! One day they just started calling themselves the "50/50 Club." These folks, along with others of different ages, gender, and culture, are landing jobs regularly from following the process.

How cool it is to see a core demographic once crippled in pride after being laid-off of work (for most, after 20-30 years) pull themselves together to find a new start. We can all learn lessons from the "50/50 Club." These people went through all the emotions of disbelief, despair, low self-esteem, and more—only to climb out of the dark clouds to try something completely unheard of. There was enough uncertainty in their lives—trying *HSE* was not an easy thing to do on top of everything else going on.

The easy way out for these non-traditional "re-career" starters would have been early retirement and a major overhaul in quality of life or grabbing the first job that came long—only to be more miserable. Rather, they took the road less traveled through *HSE*. They are better off because of that decision and a true inspiration to all of us.

Chapter 5

The envelope, please. Your ideal job starts with a blank page.

Why go back to what you had?

Your next job is whatever you want it to be! Yes, in a sluggish economy, you call the shots. Kind of funny, isn't it? Reports of record unemployment don't jive with this assertion. Jobseekers who go through the *Human Search Engine* actually turn down jobs, and you will too if you follow the **process**.

It is easier said than done, but for a moment think of being unemployed as having a blank page. It is your time to take a fresh look at what you want your next job to resemble. Invest time in understanding and documenting the skills that you performed in your previous job(s) (we call these "Achievement Statements"—to be discussed as part of the instructional process later). Reassess which skills you'd like to focus on to increase the likelihood that you will enjoy your next job.

Let's agree that wanting more money is an innate part of living for anyone, despite variances in lifestyle, basic needs, etc. Now that we have this notion in front of us as a fair contention, is it then safe to say that today's ideal job has *nothing to do with making more money*? You can't define an "ideal job" as a "high-paying job." Why? Because they're not the same.

Those who believe that making a lot of money equates to having the ideal job will never be satisfied. If your definition of reaching financial security is "more," then you'll never hit it. Under this premise, will you honestly and consistently give it your all during work? Will you truly be devoted to your company (or even your own business in a healthy way)? Do you get out of bed in the morning with a burning desire to positively make a difference in your external and internal relationships? When money controls personal and professional development, it disables one's ability to effectively nurture relationships.

The late renowned Clinical Psychologist Frederick Herzberg claimed that salary is not an effective motivator to work as one would expect. Achievement and recognition are deemed more effective motivators. In essence, achievement and recognition are brought to life through *HSE*.

Consider the earlier referenced displaced worker who couldn't wait to share who he talked to after four weeks of attending my *HSE* sessions. He had made a comfortable wage during his supervisory years at a manufacturing company. After losing his job, he concentrated more on finding a company that better appreciated his unique skills. After all, this man's yearlong search for "any job" didn't produce a single, legitimate opportunity.

With all due respect to traditional career search methods, they do usually render some sort of opportunity or two at least after a year of looking for a job—even in this economy. That wasn't the case with this displaced worker. Although he didn't land a job from a conventional approach, that doesn't mean opportunities for him weren't available. *This signifies a major point about what constitutes an ideal job.*

Herzberg espoused to the theory that a salary increase is naturally related to advancement in the workplace. In other words, a salary increase essentially accompanies a person's achievements on the job. His theory and my message to jobseekers both ascribe an ideal job to high ethical standards and working for universal advancement (that being profit for the *company* and skill set development that leads to promotion opportunities for an *individual*).

Finding a job that you like is as equally as important as landing the job itself. The integration of these two objectives makes the *HSE **process*** so worthwhile. If salary is the primary motivator to the jobseeker, then whatever type of career is attained, it won't solve the problem of discontentment.

In today's competitive job market, employee discontentment is something that a chaotic economy does not need when jobs are at a premium. So, for starters, is finding your ideal job ***just*** about making more money than ever before? If yes, then the *Human Search Engine* may not have as much relevance in your life.

I can't say how much your next job will pay. What I can say is that you control this process, so desired salary ranges will likely be part of your skilled networking anyway. Plus, remember the "50/50 Club?" That many people making more than $50,000 a year is nothing to balk at. Finally, *HSE* has many 'grads' (those who have gone through the process and have landed jobs) who are making well over $100,000 a year.

The point I'm trying to emphasize is don't accept just anything out of your next job regardless of pay, title, or a shiny new office. *HSE* will make sure you enjoy what you're going to be doing, and you will be doing it in an environment that fits your values.

Welcome to the *Human Search Engine:* Instructional Unit

This section of the book is divided into four units of step-by-step prefatory guidance and instruction to direct you toward landing a job that you will enjoy:

1. **PREPARING** you for the *HSE* process through 'priming the engine' (Chapters 6-9, precursors to instruction; Chapter 10, instructional preface)
2. **DEFINING** who you are through 'igniting the engine' (Chapters 11–14, instruction)
3. **RESEARCHING** how you will solve an employer's needs through 'idling the engine' (Chapters 15–17, instruction)
4. **MARKETING** you for any situation at any time through 'running the engine' (Chapters 18–24, instruction)

Chapter 6

Precursor 1 to the Process:
Expect the unexpected, but expect results:
How your HSE Search will likely go.

After taking people through the *Human Search Engine* hundreds of times, it has become clear to me that if people use this process, their job search journey will be very predictable. While each of my students and clients over the past 10 years is unique, their job search is not. When I tell people that I can predict how their search will go, they very often push back and say, "Yes, but you've never had someone in MY position before."

I hate to disappoint you, but your search is entirely predictable. I don't care who you are, what you do, or where you are in the country or the world. The fact that *HSE* is a process means that your search will travel the same roads as everyone else. The details of your situation will change, but the path is already laid out for you. if you do the work.

Your *HSE* search will go something like this:

1. You will try your job search first independently, discarding thoughts that you can't find employment on your own. You have landed jobs before on your own. How could this be any different? Remember, *HSE* jobs are not predicated on taking you back to careers where you were once miserable. The unique process will not allow for that to happen.

2. You will utilize all of the Internet resources that you know of to determine why your method isn't working this time.

3. You will seek help randomly without a clear goal or plan. You will end up with one or two leads and think, "Wow this networking thing works great."

4. Your contacts will lead you basically nowhere relevant, and you will begin to blame the world for your situation (there are no jobs out there, I'm too old, I'm too male/female, there are no jobs in that industry anymore, all the good jobs have been outsourced, etc.).

5. You will find or be given this book and will almost immediately not read it. Disbelief that there is an entirely different way of doing job search will keep you from reading the material.

6. After reviewing the successes of others through the *HSE* process, you will begin to talk about it. You will examine how you have found everything else of value in your life and conclude that you did it through networking.

7. You will diligently work through the book. but your efforts will be rushed or incomplete because you hope there is some miracle to this process.

8. After using this process and failing due to your lack of dedication and a diversion from the way it is sequentially outlined for your benefit, you recommit to it.

9. You start having worthwhile Informational Interviews and Networking Meetings with your ABC List (terms you will get to know very well in this book) people and discover really good results. You are sure that the job of your dreams is just a few conversations away. You even begin telling other jobseekers about the process and try to teach parts of it to them (which is a good move, by the way. but refer them to the formal process as well).

10. You become discouraged that you have not landed yet and start moving away from the needed activity level.

11. You regain momentum after someone you networked with several weeks ago contacts you out of the blue with a really great lead.

12. The lead doesn't directly turn into a job offer, but it does help you focus your newly reenergized search based on an organizational profile. You jump into networking full force and even join an Accountability Group to have others support your search.

13. You begin conducting really great meetings that seem to be leading you in the direction of landing a terrific job. These meeting are all with decision makers, and they are people who have workplace problems that need to be solved; they see you as someone who can actually solve those problems.

14. When nothing immediate happens you start to question if the people who you met with were sincere.

15. The call comes from an organization, a staffing firm, a recruiter, or from a connection as a direct result of an Informational Interview or Networking Meting that you had recently or several conversations ago. You instantly

realize that you nailed an interview or meeting because of all of your preparation and research. and are offered a position!

TAKE AWAY

Some of you are shaking your head right now. How can he (meaning I) know that. we've never even met? As with all things process related, the results are predictable. ***The only variables are your willingness to do the work and how you present yourself to the world.***

Chapter 7

Precursor 2 to the Process:
Be humble, be sincere, ask for help.

A common theme that dominates my first meeting with anyone centers around fundamentally changing a person's attitude about how he or she should present themself during a job search. In layman's terms, I need to "unlearn" for this person everything he or she THINKS they know about job search. The first thing we discuss is how they will present themselves to the world during the process.

There are a myriad of articles over a long span of time that teaches people that the best way to present themselves during a job search. These lessons suggest that jobseekers puff out their chests and confidently mesmerize those they are meeting with by telling stories about how they "greatly and almost single-handedly changed the fortunes" of an organization.

The goal (so you have been told) is to impress people so much during your interaction that they will spontaneously throw their arms around you and declare, "I can't believe we have finally found you! Can you start on Monday for $90,000 a year with four-weeks of vacation and stock options?" That is a beautiful dream. but that's all it is—a dream. I often refer to this as the "Disney ending" to your job search. You have seen it in movies, read about it in magazines, and hope with all of your heart that this is how your job search will end.

"How's that working for you?" as Dr. Phil might ask.

The fact is, you know better. You have not once ever created a meaningful relationship in your life that way, but somehow now it's going to work because some Internet job blog told you it would? Isn't it more likely that you will develop this new networking or job relationship the same way you have created every other meaningful relationship in your life? Have you ever created a new relationship by impressing people with your skills, talents, and abilities the first time the two of you met? Not likely.

Let's be clear, there will be plenty of time during the job interview phase of your job search where telling your achievement stories will be incredibly valuable. as a matter of fact, you will write out achievement narratives as part of this process for use at the right time. At this point in using the *Human Search Engine* process, we will be asking for and garnering support from others in the effort for people

WILLING to help you to get you in front of those who are ABLE to help you. We do that by using the first and most important precursor to the process.

Be humble, be sincere, ask for help.

Be humble

Try to envision the last new person who you met that was really obnoxious. There was no way the two of you were going to strike up a friendship of any type. What was it about this person? Was he/she opinionated? Did the individual work too hard to impress you with how wealthy or athletic he/she was? Did he/she not let you get a word in at all? My guess is that this person lost you in the first minute of your conversation because he/she was not humble.

While people are drawn to confidence, they run screaming from bravado. More importantly, because our intent is to ask people to assist us in our search by going over the top to tell them how great you are will likely alienate them ,or worse yet. have them asking themselves, "If they are so great, what do they need my help for?"

Just ask yourself. when was the last time you turned your back on a truly humble or genuine person? Now ask yourself. when was the last time you turned away from someone who was too full of themself? Maybe just last week?

Be sincere

As I write this, we are right in the middle of the 2012 Presidential campaign. It is about a month from the election. can you see where I'm heading with this?

I'm not sure which candidate you would identify as least sincere, but I'm guessing politicians and used car dealers would rank right up there. You can smell insincerity a mile away. As George Burns once quipped, "Once you can fake sincerity. you've got it made." *HSE* people don't fake sincerity. they are sincere. People have a pretty good 'BS' detector built right into them. Once you identify someone as insincere, they are done in your book. They are also done in their job search.

The picture of an insincere used car dealer telling a gullible car buyer that he/she will give the customer this deal today "only because I like your face" is part of our lexicon. Never try to fool anyone with being insincere because insincerity is akin to lying. and people run from it.

When we say in the *HSE* process that you are going to ask people for "advice, guidance, and feedback" on your search, we are completely sincere about that. There will be no back door resume drops and no getting in front of important people asking for advice and then trying to turn it into a job interview. People in the position to hire others have a common trait—they read people well. That's how they got into that position. Insincerity stinks like rotten fish; it's easy to spot and impossible to overcome as a first impression.

Ask for help

Many psychological studies have identified the word "help" as one of the words most likely to get people to listen and to spur them to action. The broken down car at the side of the road with its hood up is a universal request for help. Complete strangers stop their journey to grandma's house at the sight of an open hood. Why?

Even the most self-absorbed person is hard wired to respond to a request for help. Whether this individual acts on the request for help is another matter, but he/she listens. Fundraising telemarketers appeal to strangers who have never seen their face to "help" them fund a cause. The word "help" screamed out of the darkness draws well-intended strangers to the site to see how they can be of assistance. People respond to requests for help, but only if the request is reasonable and they can relate to it.

Considering that we will not be asking strangers for help, but rather asking people already WILLING to help us makes us wonder how they will respond. The request for help needs to be reasonable and they must be able to relate to it. Asking someone for help in finding a job is not a reasonable request because it is not well defined, creates a lot of work , and drops your unemployment problem in this person's lap while asking the individual to solve it. That's not networking. that's begging. Asking someone for advice on the best pizza in town is one thing; asking them to drive you there and buy the pizza for you is a different matter.

You have asked for help many times in your life. If the request was reasonable and people could relate to it, they helped you. How could asking people for help in your job search be any different? That's the cool thing about *HSE*. to judge whether the theories are true or not. Just compare them with your own life experiences.

Be humble, be sincere, ask for help. it beats the heck out of the "try and impress complete strangers strategy," doesn't it?

TAKE-AWAY

Welcome humility into your life. It's not a bad thing and it is quite self-revealing. People want to help you with your job search, but they don't know how. *HSE* participants have no choice when it comes to humility. If you follow the process honestly and diligently, you will succeed.

Chapter 8

Precursor 3 to the Process:
No one knows you exist, and you are unaware of at least 85% of companies that would hire you right now.

Rule 1: HR people can't hire you until they know you exist

Employment advisors tell you to craft the best resume and cover letter and send them to hundreds of companies "to get your name out there." Has this labor-intensified, impersonal approach in finding a job worked for you?

Getting your name "out there" doesn't work for three reasons. First, can you show me where "out there" actually is? I have seen some pretty sophisticated GPS technology, but I'm not sure these units could locate this destination known as "out there." No one knows you exist, and introducing yourself on a piece of paper along with the rest of the world won't advance your job search very far. The only person who may see your name is an HR professional for perhaps a split second. Then you will likely earn a spot in a filing cabinet or the recycle bucket. Either way, those results based on chance and luck are not where a jobseeker wants to be.

Second, innovative HR professionals aren't relying on the cover letter/resume approach as much as they once did. Why? The process is too slow, too costly, and unauthenticated. Competition for trustworthy talent today is at an all-time high in a new economy. Subsequently, HR professionals are reassessing the way they find talent because budgets are particularly tight and resources are lean.

Third, traditional jobseekers know very little or nothing at all about the companies they are randomly sending their credentials to. It's time to stop counting on a shot in the dark to produce success and happiness. We need the right people and a plan to optimize the effectiveness of networking. You send resumes in hope of gaining a face-to-face meeting. The *Human Search Engine* produces those same meetings in a more personal, purposeful, and focused way, and I can tell you that is appreciated by those who sit on the other side of the interview desk.

Rule 2: You can't work for an organization that you don't know exists

You are unaware of at least 85% of companies that would hire you right now.

For jobseekers, it is a hard enough realization that nobody knows you exist. Compound that awareness with the fact that within a 30-mile radius of the college where I work, for example, there are about 30,000 organizations. I ask my jobseekers to estimate how many of these businesses they could actually name. Between 100-150 names is usually a fair response. If a jobseeker is that unfamiliar with a general snapshot of regional employers, then imagine how many employers are unaware of where the talent pool is residing as well. HSE brings the skilled worker and employer together through the process.

> *If a jobseeker is that unfamiliar with a general snapshot of regional employers, then imagine how many employers are unaware of where the talent pool is residing as well. HSE brings the skilled worker and employer together through the process.*

About 65 – 80% of jobs are never posted through traditional advertising. Most people drive to work the same way each day, visit the same store for groceries, or even have lunch with the same people on a regular basis. Humans are creatures of habit and comfort. The bottom line, per the geographical example above, is that more than 30,000 employers don't know you exist; therefore, you are unaware of a huge number of jobs that are never posted. A company cannot hire you unless it knows you exist.

TAKE AWAY

Until you solve the two biggest job search problems (nobody knows that you exist, and you are unaware of at least 85% of companies that would hire you right now), you will continue to struggle with your search. Solving these problems through *HSE* will open up a world of opportunities for you.

Take time to give strategic networking a shot through this book and the *HSE* process. You will then be able to apply it within your daily routines. All you need are the right tools and a foundation to execute this level of networking, and *HSE* will lay the groundwork for you to make that happen.

Chapter 9

Precursor 4 to the Process:
Get to know YOU. You won't need to change yourself for anyone or for any job.

In my world, the most common cause of unhappiness at work is because people don't choose their professional passion as a career. They fall into a world of changing who they are to try and match what jobs are available. This is nothing but a train wreck; yet it is very common. Is it really a surprise to anyone that spending 2,000 hours a year doing something that <u>someone</u> else chose for them is a recipe for disaster?

Along those lines, it is becoming common practice today for companies to use assessment surveys in an attempt to capture the essence of one's personality. They are used as part of interview screening, professional development plans, and more to best match human dynamics in business. The Myers-Briggs Type Indicator is one of the more popular assessments used to define personality type.[7]

The need for personality assessments in business stems from the theory that behavior is actually orderly and consistent, according to the Myers & Briggs Foundation. The relevance of the theory offsets arguments that personalities are based on random variations of human behavior. In other words, humans possess basic differences in the ways they prefer to use their perception and judgment.

Isabel Briggs Myers, co-founder of the Myers-Briggs Type Indicator, ideally and indirectly tied her vision of the need for personality evaluation to the *Human Search Engine* process. "Whatever the circumstances of life, the understanding of (personality) type can make your perceptions clearer, your judgments sounder, and your life closer to your heart's desires." [8]

Her words juxtapose my philosophy behind the success of *Human*. The *HSE* process is predicated on a jobseeker's ability to present him or herself confidently and purposefully, while engaging in an innovative form of networking. A critical component to reaching this latter step in the process relies on the jobseeker's understanding of his or her personality type.

The *HSE* jobseeker should take the Myers-Briggs Type Indicator because its findings set the stage for optimized networking. A person's unique personality traits will leverage relationships that result from interactions made possible through *HSE*. The key is understanding who you are as a person in preparation for the most significant networking you'll ever experience.

TAKE AWAY

Don't change yourself just for a job. You cannot make it look like you can fit into any workplace dynamic. Instead, first self-discover or simply affirm who you are in the most generic of terms by taking a personality assessment, like the Myers-Briggs Type Indicator. It will provide a baseline for you to work off of as you are now about to 'ignite the engine' by defining your values, interests, and goals. There are 70-plus years of psychological research to guide your job choices once you determine your personality type and what it means.

Chapter 10

Instructional Unit Preface

Definition, **Research**, and **Marketing** make up the **instructional** content of the *Human Search Engine*. First, let's look at some basic business principles that draw an important correlation to understanding *HSE*.

When a corporation develops a product or service, it uses a three-step process that basically mirrors *HSE*. This is important for you to know from the outset. The process you are about to learn is not a new age infomercial way to find a job—its' quite the contrary. You will soon learn how to use a process that is time tested over decades. It has been used by some of the largest corporations in the world; society as a whole is just not holistically in tune with this as a concept.

The same three steps used by companies to conduct commerce globally have developed a spark for our economy through *HSE*. Let's introduce each step and see why they are powerful building blocks to market anything (in this case, it's all about marketing YOU and your skills to employers that need them).

Definition

Before we can market anything to anyone, the first step is to define what this product or service is. and is not. These are the questions that have to be answered (write them down and keep them handy as you start your *HSE* process in order to put clear definition around what is being sold or marketed. In this case, that's YOU!).

What does your product or service do?
What does it look like?
What problems does it solve?
Is there anything else like it?
What are its benefits and features that will appeal to customers?

Most importantly, can we define this product or service in a way that is easy to understand to the general public? If we make the mistake of over-defining in very technical terms, then the ability to market a product, service, or even ourselves to the general public becomes ineffective.

Research

After we have clearly defined 'what' we will be promoting to the marketplace, the next step is to do research on it and the market(s) it is to be sold into. To put this concept into a tangible, sequential context, consider these questions (and again have them handy throughout the *HSE* process):

What problems exist that people need to solve?
Who has these problems and why?
Why can't they solve those problems with their current or other tried resources?
What is the cost in time and money, in addition to negative effects, if the problems are not solved or if an opportunity is not seized?
What are people willing to pay for a solution to the problems?
Does a solution provide opportunities in other, less obvious markets as well?

Marketing

Now that we have a product or a service that is well defined and we are convinced that people need it, how do we make people aware of its availability? Consider these marketing ideas:

What advertising channels exist?
Who are the industry experts that can evaluate the value of the product or service?
How do we create word-of-mouth advertising to promote it?
How do we help people decide that they need it instead of pushing this thing on them?
Who is willing to help promote this once they know its value?
What industry specific words, phrases, or concepts need to be part of the marketing plan?
Whose endorsement or recommendation do we need?

> *Is it fair then to think that if this process works for multi-billion dollar, multi-national corporations, it is good enough for us?*

The three-category process that I have just outlined goes on in offices around the world every day. Whether someone is creating a new sports drink, an electronic gadget, or promoting a candidate for public office, the process is always the same. Is it fair then to think that if this process works for multi-billion dollar, multi-national corporations, it is good enough for us? I am not prescribing a magic pill—just a proven method that conceptually goes on around you every day in every part of your life.

It's checklist time for the engine that is known as the *Human Search Engine*:

Proven?	YES ✓
Controllable?	YES ✓
Predictable?	YES ✓
Logical?	YES ✓
Sequential?	YES ✓
Experiential?	YES ✓
Terminal (by way of success)?	YES ✓
Easy?	**NO** ✗

TAKE AWAY

When was the last time that something really worthwhile was so easy? So, let's get to work!

Chapter 11
DEFINING

What to do at 8:00 a.m. each morning.
A step-by-step guide to the new job search process.

**The *Human Search Engine*
INSTRUCTIONAL PROCESS STEP 1:**

Identify Your Achievements and Learn How to Express Them

The first step toward landing a rewarding career today is to write Achievement Statements. Consider how traditional jobseekers have captured their successes from previous jobs or job-related experiences. They listed them on a resume. Resumes are still useful, and in some cases necessary, to complete a job search. The job search playing field has changed, however, and the resume and cover letter don't pave roads to success as exclusively as they once did.

The *Human Search Engine* jobseeker, however, brings two special characteristics to the hiring process that makes employers more comfortable with whom they're first conversing with and then ultimately hiring: credibility and familiarity. The job market is more competitive than ever before—relying on a piece of paper to make what typically equates to a $500,000 decision ($50,000/year for 10 years) is not the way employers are leaning these days when it comes to hiring.

Writing Achievement Statements launches the *HSE* journey toward something better because it signifies a new way of thinking toward an old way of trying to advance your life. As a result of internalizing successes through Achievement Statements, the first part of the *HSE* process introduces each jobseeker's distinct story to an ever-revolving network of key stakeholders in landing careers. The story becomes "elevator" talking points for the jobseeker for every networking opportunity that will purposefully surface through *HSE*.

More importantly, these Achievement Statements will become the foundation on which your job search is formed. They will be the basis for your answers to interview questions. They will be the basis for the message that you give to people when you first meet them during your search. They will form your ability to

~ 43 ~

"paint a picture" of your past work in the minds of the people who you network with. and of course, they will show up on your resume and cover letter.

People want to hire individuals who think like they do and hold the same professional values and motivations. *HSE* unites these disclosures *before* any conversation ensues through its networking process. It's like an informal, pre-screening form of dialogue without the scheduling, power play settings, and other bells and whistles that accompany formal interviews.

Here's what to do to begin the *Human Search Engine* journey:

A. In detail, write 7–10 work achievements that you are most proud of or brought the most value to your organization. Focus on achievements where you played an integral role in making them happen. This is no time for modesty. Your past achievements are the best indication that a future employer has on how you can solve its problems, make its life easier, and get it closer to attaining important goals.

B. Turn each achievement into a *short* story. Do it in a way so a person who was not there during that event can understand the situation by putting him or herself in the same setting. Focus on three important areas:

1. What did you do?

Bring to light your high-level responsibilities, not titles and tasks. For example, disclose that you were responsible as a leader for overseeing the lifestyles and safety of more than 150 assisted living residents at Breezy Lane Home for Elderly, in addition to expanding the organization's residency through record sales. This delivers more punch than saying, "I served as the resident manager for Breezy Lane Home for the Elderly."

We have one breath to cast an impression on someone. Words like lifestyles, safety, leader, and growth are attached with someone who must be skilled—more so than just "manager." Make sure that the statement is made in terms that even people who are not from your industry can easily understand it.

2. How did you do it?

The most important step for today's jobseekers is their ability to describe how they performed on any given job through bringing skills to life. It's natural to say, "I have strong writing skills." Albeit that may be a truthful and forthright statement, how about saying, "My former company used my writing skills to publish more than 2,000 press releases last year in a variety of media, helping establish new target markets for its products while generating enhanced visibility."

Most jobseekers hone in on getting the results of their work (the last of this three-part Achievement Statement writing process) across to someone first. Results are measurably significant in portraying a jobseeker's credentials, but consider *when* in the process this disclosure is to be unveiled. More importantly, "how you did it" supersedes this point for the successful *HSE* jobseeker, again, because the process is skill-based.

While every potential employer is going to hear about results, how fundamentally involved were you in the positive outcomes of a given project? Consider a continuation from the above example at Breezy Lane Home for the Elderly: "I gathered a task force at the Home and led a new marketing strategy that concentrated on providing on-the-spot tours for visitors, instead of scheduling the tours as a next step phase of a visit."

This example displays how one person expanded the organization's occupancy (which is the number one means of profit in this business) through implementing a change in marketing procedures. In this instance, the jobseeker used negotiation, marketing, planning, organization, and leadership skills.

Other common skills that would be identified from your achievements might include problem solving, project management, sales and promotion, team building, creating a process, leading people, gathering data, mechanical skills, customer service, operating equipment, teaching or training, organizing, troubleshooting, etc.

Once a set of skills is identified, jobseekers can easily recreate an event of major relevancy in their pursuit of a rewarding career. Consequently, potential employers realize that your skills can work for them as well!

Be sure to focus on skills that directly create value for an organization. What were people paying you to do in order to solve their problems, make their life easier, and get them closer to their next goal? You will discover more on specific skills in the next chapter.

3. *What was the result?*

The best results will be measurable and easy to substantiate. Focus on time or money saved as high-level outcomes to share. Here are examples:

- Sales increases or the ability to create larger sales
- Increasing levels of responsibility
- Increased efficiency or reduced waste
- Creating new business relationships or partnerships
- Opening up new markets
- Removing internal or external conflicts or obstacles

It is important that your results can draw a direct line between your efforts and the positive outcome.

Again, we want to share results with potential channels to hiring, but it's advantageous to do so through sharing stories—by painting a picture. That's why, as noted above, it's imperative to depict scenes that describe how you were fundamentally instrumental in the results—not just "involved" in them. Everyone focuses on results in this manner—by coming across as they were "a part of" or "involved" in something. Think about it. That's a rather passive approach toward selling skills.

Another way to think of these achievement stories is to write them as if you were preparing answers for an interview (you can start to see how these stories will become useful throughout the process).

Describe the situation you were in (What was your position or role? What type of organization or industry were you in? Were you managing people, a process, or doing the actual work?).

Describe the problem or opportunity that you addressed (What was the issue? How did you become aware of it? Were you responsible directly for carrying it through or serving as an active member of a team? What was the negative or anticipated consequence of not acting?).

Describe your actions to solve the problem or act on the opportunity (What options did you have? How did you decide on a course of action? What actions did you decide on and why? Did you act alone or did you act as part of a team? How did you implement your actions, and how was success measured?).

Describe the positive results of your actions (Were there increased sales or decreased costs? Were efficiencies improved? Was an employee developed? Were processes put in place? Did you find a new market?).

Each Achievement Statement should be about one page long and contain enough detail to convey to the receiver of your conversation two key points. First, you need to "place them as if they were there when your achievement occurred." *Second*, you need to use detailed, yet simple, language so the receiver understands enough about the industry you worked in. Don't use sophisticated words to over-impress; you'll only turn the person off (unless you're absolutely positive the other person has a very high-level knowledge of your industry).

Here is an opportunity not to scrimp on key details. Write these statements and

> *We can have all the networking opportunities in the world, but unless you can share with people how to solve their problems, make their life easier, or help get them closer to the next bonus or sale, then networking is nothing more than a lovely conversation.*

rehearse them as if you were talking to a complete stranger, because when you use this information in a networking or interview setting, **you likely will be talking to a stranger!**

This first *HSE* step serves as the foundation to connect with someone who may be tied to an employer through presenting your **skills** in a story (again, not just saying I am a skilled communicator, for instance). It is an "elevator" speech of who you are. The story piece serves as an example of what you did, how you did it, and any given results of those actions. It is a "show" not a "tell."

We can have all the networking opportunities in the world, but unless you can share with people how to solve their problems, make their life easier, or help get them closer to the next bonus or sale, then networking is nothing more than a lovely conversation.

Here is another helpful example that is provided from start-to-finish through the summary of **what did you do, how did you do it, and what was the result?**

I was responsible for all aspects regarding the installation and start-up of a $3 million paper converting line **(what I did)**. I evaluated the situation by bringing together the machine manufacturer, the construction company that was setting the machine in place, and the operating staff who would be running the machine. I created a timeline for installation, identified tasks to be completed, and then assigned them to responsible parties with completion dates. Along the way, I instituted a weekly update meeting that included all responsible parties to discuss the project's progress and to make any necessary modifications **(how I did it)**.

The paper converting machine started up on time, within cost, and met a predetermined start-up production curve **(the result)**.

Before you read any further, start working on your Achievement Statements! Our goal is face-to-face meetings with people in your industry. we need stories to tell upon arrival!

TAKE AWAY

Step 1 of the *HSE* process builds a foundation for the jobseeker to tell stories about relevant experiences in the workplace by *writing Achievement Statements* and learning how to summarize them.

.

Chapter 12

DEFINING

The *Human Search Engine* INSTRUCTIONAL PROCESS STEP 2:

Identify Skills from Your Achievements

The previous and first step of the *Human Search Engine* process established a baseline for jobseekers to articulate how they solved problems. In other words, what did they do that was noteworthy in their positions? Achievements serve as the catalyst behind step one, and those results begin to fill a pipeline of substantive content for the *HSE* jobseeker.

The *HSE* process focuses on identifying fundamental skills for the jobseeker. These skills become a major piece of *HSE* networking exchanges (opportunities that play out later in the overall process). When expressed in alignment with strategic tactics of *HSE* networking that will be presented later in this book, these skills will convince key individuals to help you shape and find a new career.

Now, create a list from your achievement experiences that identify skills you have used in the workplace. Consider what skills were used to contribute toward each of your previously noted achievements. Below is a sample list of professional skills created by a former marketing manager at a large insurance firm:

- Communication (oral, formal public speaking, written, etc.)
- Editing (copy, writing, scripting, etc.)
- Management (project, people, etc.)
- Marketing (research, target or online marketing, focus groups, advertising, etc.)
- Planning
- Supervising

Here are some other skills commonly used in association with various business-related achievements:

- Analysis
- Budgeting
- Coordination
- Cost-savings

Design (industrial, mechanical, interior, commercial, product, graphic/computer, etc.)

Development (product, service, construction, fundraising, event, etc.)

Diagnostic

Established (system, process, procedure, event, form of recognition, policy, etc.)

Figure/Calculate (a problem, a solution, etc.)

Instructed/Trained

Leadership (any reference to leading people or a process, project, etc.)

Negotiated

Programmed (processes, software, systems, networks, etc.)

Researched (problems, case studies, improved processes, products, services, etc.)

Sold

Troubleshoot

Refer back to the Achievement Statements that you wrote. Assign the appropriate skills that you just listed to each one of the Achievement Statements. You will begin to see certain skills that show up in most of these Achievement Statements. There is a pattern developing. You are beginning to form the skills that will be part of your next career position. Yes, you are defining that position as we speak.

As an *HSE* jobseeker, you will use a Venn diagram (see image below) to organize your skills. Here are the steps for the development of your Venn diagram (you can simply use the visual as a model to draw your own Venn diagram on a separate piece of paper—make sure to LABEL them as follows):

- In one circle, list the skills you're good at.
- In another circle, list the skills you love to do.
- In the final circle, list the skills you are paid to do.
- Now find the skills that were listed in at least two of the circles. This is the intersection of the circles (intersection highlighted).

To put this list in perspective, you may be good at some skills, but at the same time, you may not enjoy using them. For example, consider negotiation skills. You may excel at the art of negotiation, yet your stress levels fly through the ceiling when you have to use this skill, causing sleepless nights. Conversely, you may love working on computer-based designs, yet those are not the competencies you are being paid for.

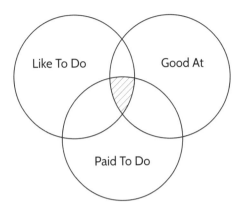

Once you complete filling in the Venn diagram, examine the intersection of the three circles. What you're looking at is a job in any shape or form for any industry in which those intersected skills make up 90% of what you will do in your next job. Identifying these skills is simple and purposeful, plus it comes from you. It is a self-managed step in the *HSE* **process** that lets you call the shots to land your next career—one in which you will also feel valued and fulfilled.

One of the biggest mistakes people make when looking for a job is they present themselves to be "anyone a potential employer wants them to be." Don't approach your next job with desperation; instead, take it on with skill. If you don't allow skill to direct your career path, the result is often accepting the first job that comes along. How can a jobseeker blame anyone but himself/herself if this job turns out to be a bad choice? Follow the *HSE* process and that will not happen.

TAKE AWAY

If you don't know where you're going, any road can get you there. Understanding your skills through the Venn diagram and how you can position them to solve problems for someone else is a big advantage and a major tool of the *Human Search Engine*. Now, refine the skills out of your achievements, and put them in the three-circled Venn diagram. **What skills does it make sense to focus your job search around, moving forward?**

> *One of the biggest mistakes people make when looking for a job is they present themselves to be "anyone a potential employer wants them to be."*

Chapter 13
DEFINING

The *Human Search Engine* INSTRUCTIONAL PROCESS STEP 3:

ID Jobs that use Your Skills

Through the Venn diagram process, you should now have a sharper understanding of the ideal skills that will define your next job. Now, you can focus on expanding the scope of the jobs that need your skills. This is a point when I see one of the biggest revelations from jobseekers of the *Human Search Engine*. A jobseeker's view of the world goes from. there's nothing out there. to wow, where do I start? Remember, in general terms jobseekers are unaware of 60-85% of the jobs that are available.

With a clear set of skills in mind, now create a list of "jobs" that require your talents. Let's look at an example below of the Venn diagram that is a result of an *HSE* jobseeker who did the three-step process. At its three-layered intersection of common identifiers, assume that the Venn diagram pinpoints the following skills of the jobseeker: researching, writing, training, and public speaking.

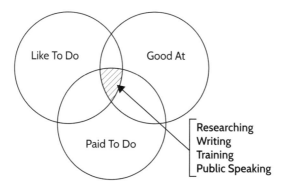

In this example, the jobseeker was a quality manager at a manufacturing company in his previous line of work. As a traditional jobseeker, he would likely pursue his next career by concentrating on words and concepts like *quality* and *management* (right from his title). Conversely, what you as an *HSE* jobseeker would do in this instance is center your attention on a job that can use any or all of the skills pertaining to researching, writing, training, and public speaking.

HSE expands the breadth of job options as a result of these Venn-identified skills. You now realize you can work as a college instructor, a grant writer, a non-profit programming specialist or executive director, a corporate trainer, a marketing research professional, or a research and development director, to name a few.

An exercise that will help you determine what types of positions value your skills is the **Five Job Postings Exercise:**

1. View the skills that you have identified as your strengths (the intersection of the Venn diagram).
2. Search job postings using one of those skills as a key word search item. From the example above, one of these skills might be **training** (or use any skill that you'd like).
3. Go to the search area of any one of the large national job search sites. There you will see a spot where you can enter a keyword, and the program will search the database to find which jobs have that word in the job description.
4. Enter **training** in the search field that indicates "search by skill."

> *This is a point when I see one of the biggest revelations from jobseekers of the Human Search Engine. A jobseeker's view of the world goes from there's nothing out there to wow, where do I start? Remember, in general terms jobseekers are unaware of 60-85% of the jobs that are available.*

Training may appear in job postings for trainer, consultant, coach, coordinator, or specialized areas like safety, management, technical development, etc. The fact that many different jobs use this skill will begin to open your eyes to career possibilities that you may not have considered.

Don't limit yourself to local jobs either as part of this activity. You are just doing research, so if you live in Texas, but find a job posting for a position in Ohio. no problem. You are not going to apply to the job in Ohio, but maybe careers like this exist within 10 or 20 miles of where you live now. Becoming aware of possibilities you hadn't considered is the goal of this exercise.

You need to broaden your scope of what is out there as far as possibilities. Consider industries that you have never thought of before. After all, this a research project. You will begin to see that your skills are valued by many different companies, by many different industries, and in many different job titles.

That's the freedom of the *HSE* process. it's all about possibilities. There will be plenty of time to investigate each of the jobs that interest you during the research phase, which begins in the next chapter. Perhaps for the first time in a long time you will be asking yourself, "What do I want?" instead of, "What should I take?" The latter question is an empty and desperate feeling because you feel there are limited opportunities.

The last part of the definition phase of *HSE* is for you to come up with several clear objectives in which you will start your search. This is referred to as an Objective Statement. Your Objective Statement will take this format:

"A _____ position involving _____ , _____ , and _____ for a(n) _____ company focused on _____."

Example: "A <u>lean facilitator</u> position involving <u>identifying and eliminating waste</u>, <u>implementing Six Sigma strategies</u>, and <u>conducting kaizen events</u> for a <u>progressive manufacturing</u> company focused on <u>world class products</u>."

Notice two aspects about the above Objective Statement example:

- Industry-specific words are used in the Objective Statement so that people from the field will quickly identify your expertise. These words indicate to people a level of knowledge about the industry and a competency that you have served in that field.
- The Objective Statement allows the person who you are networking with to immediately identify in his or her "mental Rolodex" (a term used when referring to how many people a certain person is connected to in a top-of-mind context) the kinds of people and organizations that they know with similar backgrounds. This person can then draw recollections and/or install scripted knowledge in his or her mind for near- future interactions of others who speak similarly to you or "live in that world." It works.

Here is one other example of an Objective Statement per the blank model above: "A <u>sales manager</u> position involving <u>identifying market segment opportunities</u>, <u>teaching needs-based selling techniques</u>, and <u>increasing lead penetration through aggressive new customer prospecting</u> for an <u>international consumer goods</u> company focused on <u>outstanding customer service</u>."

Now, write two possible Objective Statements based on the skills and experience that you have identified through the *HSE* process thus far. After developing your objectives, test them on a few people who you already know to see if they can name anyone or even companies representing that kind of work. Don't worry about asking them to connect you to anyone yet. Just see if your objectives lead these people who are WILLING to help you with your search identify others in their "mental Rolodex" who might be ABLE to help you with your search.

TAKE AWAY

This last step of the defining phase is when *HSE* jobseekers start buying into the *HSE* process. It is also a real confidence builder for them. You are now taking skills that you love to do, every day, all day, and placing them in buckets that you can carry to wherever your next career is waiting. What a way to take control of your life through researching the Five Job Postings Exercise and developing and practicing Objective Statements!

Chapter 14

UNIT RECAP: Defining

1. Use an online tool to understand your Myers-Briggs Type Indicator profile.

2. Write out in detail 7-10 work-related achievements. Based on your experience these could also be education-related or volunteer experiences. These achievements should be written out in the format of: What did you do, how did you do it, and what was the result. These statements should contain significant detail to fill a page or more in length. Focus mostly on the "How did you do it" section.

3. Use the checklist from Chapter 10 to identify which specific skills were used in making each of these achievements happen. Make a specific and inclusive list of all skills used in each achievement as these will be important in the next steps.

4. Make a list of each of the skills that show up in at least half of the achievements.

5. Create the three-circle intersecting Venn diagram as shown in Chapter 12. Label the circles in the diagram as Good at doing, Love to do, and Paid to do.

6. Take the list of skills that show up in at least half of your achievements and evaluate each one of them by writing it in any of the circles that apply (Good at doing, Love to do, and Paid to do). Now find which skills fall in at least two of the three circles. This represents the "skill set" that will guide the type of job or work that you will focus on going forward in the *HSE* process.

7. Visit a large online job search engine and identify five jobs that interest you while completely ignoring how much they pay, where they are geographically, or whether you are actually qualified to do them. Print these out and now identify the words or phrases that draw you to this job. Take note of the duties and responsibilities in these positions. They

reflect the duties and responsibilities that need to be part of your next position.

8. Create two Objective Statements using industry specific terminology as presented in Chapter 13.

9. Test your Objective Statements on people who you already know. Do they make sense to them? Do they lead these people to ideas of others who "live in the world you want to live in?"

Chapter 15
RESEARCH

**The *Human Search Engine*
INSTRUCTIONAL PROCESS STEP 4:**

Finding Who Values Your Skill Set

Now that you have a good grip on the types of skills that you want to be doing every day in your next position, it is important to identify who values those skills. The core of any sales training will tell you that a sale is made when the benefits of a product or service are shown to solve the problem of the customer. Match one with the other and you won't have to sell anything to anyone; the customer will CHOOSE to buy! Job search done the *Human Search Engine* way is no different.

There are two steps within this research chapter of the *HSE* process: 1) Identifying job types and industries that value your skill set, and 2) Identifying problems in those jobs that you are uniquely able to solve.

Identifying job types and industries that value your skill set.

This is the moment when I begin to challenge what you THINK you know about the job opportunities that are around you. Take a look at the skill set that you developed through the Venn diagram. These are the skills that you will be using 90% of the time in your next position. Let's go see if we can find them in organizations around you. even ones that you have never considered or heard of.

Like we did earlier, I am going to again direct you to any of the popular job search sites on the Internet. Now, in the keyword search area of whatever job search site you selected, enter one of the skills that you came up with for yourself. like negotiation. Make sure that the site is searching in your local area code, or close to it. Type "negotiation" into the keyword search pane and hit enter.

What types of positions do you see? What types of industries do those open positions represent? Did the search also bring up names of companies that you have never heard of? What other responsibilities does that position require, and do you have those skills?

Now enter your another skill into the search pane on the job search site. Ask yourself the same questions as in the previous example with the skill of negotiation. Which other industries and companies are you becoming aware of as a result of this exercise?

Let's draw two important conclusions from the first of two steps in this research chapter.

First, you will see that some organizations are currently looking for people with your skills. Second, you became aware of many companies and organizations that you have never heard of. Remember, one of the biggest problems jobseekers have is that they are unaware of at least 85% of all of the companies within 30 miles of them. You can't work for an organization that you don't know exists.

This step in the process will begin to make you aware of hundreds of organizations around you. In my seminars, I often ask people how many organizations exist within 30 miles of Appleton, Wisconsin. The guesses range from 500 to 5,000. The actual number is more than 30,000! That fact is met with startled looks of disbelief.

Then I ask people to start naming all of those organizations. In a room full of 100 people who have lived in Appleton their whole lives, including me, we can rarely name more than 50. that's right, we miss 29,950 possible organizations. The point is made. what is out there that you (and most other jobseekers) don't know exists as employment possibilities? Remember, smart employers (to be discussed later) aren't posting positions like they used to through traditional advertising—including the Web.

> *Remember, one of the biggest problems jobseekers have is that they are unaware of at least 85% of all of the companies within 30 miles of them. You can't work for an organization that you don't know exists.*

In the process of identifying these jobs, you will also begin to notice that your skill set is valued in more than one industry. Jobseekers have an almost knee jerk reaction that leads them to return to the industry that they came from, but skill sets cross industry lines. As a former operations manager in the paper industry, I now know that the skills I used to manage production would have been valued in the production of eye glasses, cell phones, or car tires. The ability to manage teams of people, increase productivity, reduce waste, and improve safety continues to be valued by every manufacturing company around.

The same could be said for the ability to sell, design, teach, or do accounting. You will quickly find that the only one holding you in the box of returning to the same industry. is you. More industries equal more companies, and that means you will land your next position through the *Human Search Engine*.

Identifying problems that you are uniquely able to solve

Never forget that hiring managers hire people to solve their problems, make their life easier, and get them closer to their goals. In order to present yourself in a way that is attractive to an employer, you must define how you can create value for them.

Look to your Achievement Statements for problems that you have solved in the past. Do other industries value solving those problems as well? Which companies struggle with the same types of issues? Does your work save time, create sales opportunities, build teams, organize initiatives, or manage projects, to name a few?

Consider the company you last worked for. now look at its customers, competitors, and vendors. These organizations will likely value your skills as well. Are you beginning to see how your view of the workplace world is now expanding from a tunnel to the Grand Canyon? You are starting to look at job search as a bigger picture.

Now it's time to talk to the people who live in the world you want to live in. Before jumping in with no game plan to engage in this relevant dialogue, let's examine for a moment why someone from any organization would **NOT WANT to help you?** Isn't it just presumed that if you ask anyone in this context for advice that they'll give it?

I'm not saying that people are mean and don't want to help, but these types of individuals are also busy and have very little motivation to hire you more than the next guy or gal based on blanket request for "help." For starters, people cannot begin to help if all you're telling them is that 'you're really smart at everything and will do anything for any amount of money.'

This adage is the single biggest mistake jobseekers make. Look at this method of job search from the other persons' points of view—the ones who you meet with through the *HSE* process. If what they're hearing is that you are "smart" and can do anything for anyone for any amount of money, then how can they help you? It already sounds like you have all the answers, except for the one that matters most to hiring professionals: What specifically will you do for this company to solve its problems?

The people who hear a jobseeker's unfocused try at networking already have a mental Rolodex of hundreds of individuals. There is nothing significant to absorb during an exchange, and it offers no distinction from others who have offered the same jargon. You are "just a number" in the minds of someone who can open or close the next big door of a career opportunity. Why would you receive any help?

Conversely, why would someone from any organization **WANT to help you?** As an *HSE* jobseeker, you can develop Focus Statements *targeted to make people need your skills*. Managers, vice-presidents, and presidents of companies, or the primary decision-makers of any business, *are already finding their key people the same way an HSE jobseeker is going about finding a career.*

Ironic? Not really. The parallel has always been evident, just not well known. Global competition is also forcing companies to change their recruitment practices to save money and hire faster, all while receiving third-party confirmation of good talent. And it's free!

Think about good leaders of today's businesses. More than ever, they are relying on skilled professionals who are invested in a company's mission and future. These leaders too want to keep their jobs and advance the business' goals for many reasons, personally and professionally. Why would they not rely on an *HSE* method of recruitment? Again, it's free, takes little time, and produces great results. What's almost certain is that more and more businesses are going to utilize *HSE* in our ever-changing, ever-increasingly competitive job market.

At this point in the *HSE* process, we can now assume our jobseekers are well-positioned with a strategic approach that gives them a leg up against traditional job candidates. The *HSE* jobseeker is desired by companies that hire innovatively and intelligently. These companies bet on sure things.

How do *HSE* jobseekers find these companies salivating for their talent? For starters, they create what's known as an **ABC List.** When you make this list in just a moment, do so with a free mindset. Take some time to make it as comprehensive as you can. It will soon become a working list of people you know that have **hiring authority** in any industry or **own a business** (A List), **currently work in the industry you want to work in, but have no hiring authority** (B List), and **represent anyone who is willing to discuss your job search with you** (C List).

Before you start your lists, gather contacts from your email, your church, past employers and co-workers, neighbors, etc. Don't judge or evaluate the names you write—just brainstorm. We will evaluate and organize these contacts later in the process.

Now, start by creating your A List of **people who have hiring authority or own a business:**

NOTE: Chances are, as an *HSE* jobseeker you will not meet with an A List person until very late in the landing process, or perhaps never at all. It's important, though, to have A List individuals in mind. They are decision-makers and someone else you talk to may know this same person. You are likely not going to ask any of these A List people to help you get a job. so relax. It's a good thing.

If you execute the plan as it is designed, your A List individuals will understand exactly what you are doing because they wouldn't do their job search any other way! Also, think about small business owners. Do they understand networking? You bet! They don't have thousands of dollars a month to spend on advertising. If they don't network for customers, their business dies.

Once your A List is complete, now develop a B List of **people who currently work in the industry you want to work in,** *but have no hiring authority:*

NOTE: The easy conversation for you is right here with this cohort group of people from the B List. These people can relate to your skills and are not threatened to have a conversation with you because they can't hire you anyway. Individuals on your B List will provide invaluable feedback on the industry and serve as key connections to A List folks.

The fact that these people have no hiring authority is an important point here. You don't have to worry about putting pressure on them to get you a job, because they don't have the authority to give you one! What they have is industry information and connections, which is what you really need from them. Focus on former co-workers, vendors, customers, and professional colleagues.

Once your A and B Lists are complete, create the C List based on **anyone who is willing to discuss your job search with you:**

Note: The only real standard here is that these people on your C List are incredibly WILLING to help you with your search, like friends, neighbors, former co-workers, other workplace colleagues, etc. The question is, "Who thinks you're awesome?" These people want to help you with your search, but they currently don't know how. We are going to teach them how to help you!

The **ABC List** integrates two important elements for jobseekers to attain success in landing a career: 1) A pool of people who are *WILLING* to help you find a job, and 2) people who are *ABLE* to hire you. A common mistake of any jobseeker is to run to A List type-people and ask them for a job. What's in it for the executive-level individual? Why would he or she hire you? This person certainly doesn't know you or anything about your skills.

The 1000/1000 List: Start easy and start close to home

After you have created your ABC List, there is another inventory of people who I would like you to capture. Don't worry, this will be a very short list. probably three or four people at the most.

The idea for the 1000/1000 List comes from my brother, Colonel Joe Czarnik of the United States Army. Joe is certainly one of the most dedicated soldiers who you will ever meet. My brother has spent the better part of 30 years leading people in the Army in both combat and non-combat operations. Joe is a great soldier and a great leader.

He and I both went to boot camp and graduated from the Wisconsin Military Academy together as new 2nd Lieutenants. To say that we know each other is an understatement. He is actually one of my 1000/1000 List people.

His theory is simple: In life you will have LOTS of acquaintances, but very few real friends. Where do we draw the line between the two? Who will really be there for you when the "chips are down?" The answer is the 1000/1000 List.

This is the definition of your 1000/1000 List:

If you were 1000 miles away from home, in jail, on Christmas Eve and needed $1000 bail—who could you call and without a moment's hesitation, this person would grab his or her checkbook, jump in the car on Christmas Eve to come bail you out?

This is a pretty short list, isn't it? If you are like most people, you will be able to count the number of these individuals on one hand. Later in the book we will discuss starting your job search by talking to people who are most WILLING to help you.

You have just created a list of the first people you will meet with, and it's not all intimidating. This means you won't be meeting with strangers. start easy, start close to home, but start today.

Who thinks you're AWESOME?

I would like you to make one last list as we begin to think about the people who will be instrumental in your job search. I'd like you to make a list by asking yourself a simple question, "Who thinks you are awesome?"

You want to continuously get advice guidance and feedback during your search. It's best to start with people who ALREADY know that you will be an awesome find for someone as a new employee. You want to list people who are already impressed by your professional skill set. Start with people who are already on your side and know you fit the bill as a sound professional.

Make this list from several different categories:

- Former bosses or co-workers (they already know you would be a great hire—they have worked with you!)
- People from your church or civic organizations
- People who you volunteer with
- Former and current neighbors
- People who you have mentored or helped in the past
- Teachers or instructors
- Family members who you have assisted in the past

- People who you attended school with

Make this list without trying to identify how talking with each of them will get you closer to your next job. just brainstorm. Don't evaluate them based off of the last time you spoke together. Just make the list.

Again, our goal is to focus solely on people who are WILLING to help you on your search even if you have no idea how they will be ABLE to help you.

Take Away: It is imperative to find companies that value your skills instead of trying to be everything to everyone during a job search. Most job-landing *HSE* participants used the **ABC List** and other related lists as guides to mobilizing key resources to get the word out about their skills. You will soon find this same list to be a navigable tool in keeping you focused on how to most effectively spread the word to those who can get you employed.

Chapter 16

RESEARCH

**The *Human Search Engine*
INSTRUCTIONAL PROCESS STEP 5:**

What companies are out there that need your skills?
Out of these organizations, where do you now want to work?

Before we can identify where we want to go in the future, it is important for us to analyze where we have come from. It is said, "those who do not learn from the past are destined to relive it." This is so very true of jobseekers. It is time to analyze your last position to help define what you want from your next position.

If you were completely happy in your last position (but were perhaps displaced), then your search should be relatively easy. Just identify the customers, competitors, and vendors associated with that company. These customers, competitors, and vendors will likely have the same types of problems and opportunities that your last company had. That is a relatively easy list to make. Make sure, however, that you truly enjoyed that position before completing this list.

But what if you were unhappy in your last position and want to make sure that you don't end up in a similar place? If that's the case, it's time for you to define the job and situation that you are looking for in your next career.

If you were unhappy in your last job, one of three assertions has to be TRUE:

- You were in the right job, but the wrong situation
- You were in the wrong job, but the right situation
- You were in the wrong job and the wrong situation

Let's define the terms noted above in the three instances of being unhappy in a previous job:

Your "job" as stated above refers to the duties, tasks, and responsibilities of your last position. What were you functionally doing each day? What was expected of you, and what actions did you need to take to fulfill those expectations? You could also refer to the terms that were discussed earlier that we refer to as 'what skills did you use each day to accomplish your tasks?'

Your "situation" refers to the setting in which you were doing your job. It refers to the mission, values, and actions of your last employer. In other words, what was the internal dynamic like in regard to people and practices (remember my "situation" at Haldane)? What beliefs did your last employer hold? Was his/her employee assets valued, or was the staff not valued much at all?

Here is a sample portrayal from the first instance: If you were a salesperson who loves doing sales (right job), but were working for a company with deceptive sales practices (wrong situation), it would lead to stress and unhappiness in your job.

Here is a sample portrayal from the second instance: If you were working for a great organization that highly valued its employees (right situation), but you were doing mechanical repairs each day even though you had no desire to do those repairs (wrong job), then you would again find yourself in a very stressful place for different reasons. For the third instance of being in the wrong job and wrong situation, I think we can all relate to that one without providing an example!

Before researching possible employers you might want to work for, it is critical to be able to define a career that is BOTH the right job and the right situation for you. Running from the manufacturing industry (which you loved-right job) because you had a horrible boss (wrong situation) will drive you from a profession that you like and are good at just because of a bad supervisor. If this was the case, your job search research project would be all about finding a manufacturer to work for that was known for valuing its employees.

Start asking yourself these questions as part of the research component of the *Human Search Engine*. These will be the questions that you will seek to answer during the *HSE* process:

- Who in my opinion has the best job I have ever seen and that I have interest in?
- What are the really great companies to work for in the area based on feedback from employees who work there and/or from companies that do business with them?
- How do people get to work for one of those really good companies?

Lastly, I want to make this point. Often when I am working with new students or clients to identify why they left their last job or where they are headed (career-wise), I need to ask them a simple question: "With this new job, are you moving toward something good, or are you running away from something bad (like your last job)?" Honestly answering this question will keep you from accepting the first opportunity that comes your way if it doesn't fit.

Now, write a description of the "right job in the right situation" for a career you are seeking. Don't relive the past. reinvent it! Keep it handy with all of your other *HSE* tools as we continue to build your next career.

Research tools and databases to create target lists of companies:

In solving the second problem of job search (you are unaware of at least 85% of available job opportunities), there are tools at your local library that will enable you to expand your scope of job search possibilities. The key to unlocking these tools is a little thing called SIC (Standard Industrial Classification) codes.

Simply start by asking a librarian to show you the research materials that are available for jobseekers. Libraries are not archaic, folks. Today's libraries are a wealth of resources thanks to technology and inter-connective functionality with other learning resource centers designed to bridge information instantaneously. Librarians conduct research for a living. ask them for help!

Have your librarian guide you to databases such as Hoover's and Reference USA (online data bases) or your state's manufacturing and service guides (published resource books on the library shelves). Whether you are searching for companies using an online database or looking in a hard cover book, the goal is the same. You are now identifying companies that you never knew existed in your industry or area of expertise. That's where SIC codes come in.

So, now you realize there are thousands, perhaps tens of thousands, of businesses within 30 miles of your home. This is both a blessing and a curse. The blessing is that there are a lot of organizations that you haven't considered working for because you didn't know they existed. The curse is. where do you start sorting through these 20,000 or so companies? The use of SIC codes solves this problem for you.

These codes are assigned by the government to each section of the economy for purposes of categorizing organizations into groups. Every body shop has the same SIC code. Every college has the same SIC code. Every computer repair shop has the same SIC code, and so on.

Do you now see why this is so important to your search? Before you can start identifying all of the target companies that value your skill set, you need to know the SIC codes of those types of businesses. Once you know the SIC code, you can go online to find a list of all of the companies that are categorized under that classification.

In the Appleton, Wisconsin region for example, better known as the Fox River Valley or in business terms, the New North, manufacturing is big business. This region makes up the third-largest manufacturing sector in the United States. There are about a half of dozen well-known paper manufacturing companies that exist within 30 miles of my home, but there are dozens of smaller companies that represent the same industry. Most people have never heard of these smaller businesses or even considered them as potential job search targets.

The SIC code for paper manufacturing and converting is 2621. If I look under that SIC code in one of the business databases, I will see more than 70 organizations within 30 miles of my home. If my expertise is in paper manufacturing, I better know all of the companies that could use my services before I start my search. Every jobseeker is going to run to the paper companies that everyone already knows exists. Only *HSE* jobseekers will be approaching great paper companies that most people have never heard of. and those businesses may easily have great jobs that most people have never heard of either.

The next step in the *HSE* research process is creating a profile for the company you want to work for. If you create a profile of organizations that you are looking to talk with, you make it very easy for others to identify people or companies that fit that profile. Again, getting people who you are networking with to be able to narrow down the 500 people and 100 organizations that they have in their "mental Rolodex" is key. This is how, in part, you will receive direct referrals from them. In order to empower people who are WILLING to help you become ABLE to help you, creating this profile is a critical step.

> *Every jobseeker is going to run to the paper companies that everyone already knows exists. Only HSE jobseekers will be approaching great paper companies that most people have never heard of, and those businesses may easily have great jobs that most people have never heard of either.*

In your profile you must define:

- The size of the organization in terms of either gross sales or number of employees
- Is the organization privately held or publicly held?
- Is the organization a service or manufacturing organization (or other)?
- What industries do they mainly serve?
- Is it a for-profit or non-profit organization?

Once you create a profile of companies that you want to learn more about in your search, you have taken a huge step in identifying which organizations are real possibilities for employment. Now, before you move on, create a profile of the organization you want to work for next (yes, your dream job). Definition is the key. remember the old saying, "If you don't know where you are going, any road will get you there."

'The organization' that you want to work for has now been defined, philosophically and conceptually. Now this knowledge needs to be broadened to see what exists by creating a Target List.

A Target List includes all of the organizations within your geographical region (or beyond, if desired) that you would either **like to work for** or **have the skills and abilities that your next employer needs.** It's irrelevant if these companies have current posted job openings or not. Create the Target List. Aim for at least 20 organizations, for starters.

Here are some helpful tips when developing your Target List:

- List all organizations that you already know fit your professional objective
- Ask people who do the kind of work that you want to do for names of their competitors (sounds funny, but think about it. they'll either not blink an eye and give you some names, or they'll think twice about maybe wanting to explore your credentials)
- Share your Target List project with individuals on your ABC List and seek their input
- Ask friends and family for companies they have worked for or have done business with
- Research companies by using manufacturing and service directories (referenced above)
- Request employer reports and employment resources from your local college community or technical college (many people don't realize that a large repository of companies that regularly hire exist at this level of higher education due to two-year colleges' core mission of training for employment and their direct relationship to employers)

Now, research each company on your Target List to see how they are doing, what they are doing, and how they do business. The goal here is to discover enough information about each one that you could have a *quality conversation* about the company with anyone. This research will also help you determine which of these companies has values and goals that match your principles. When you have done this research, prioritize your Target List in the order of which companies you would most like to work for, or at least talk with.

Visit the company's Web site, ask your ABC List individuals about any company, Google a company to see if it was in the news recently and why, and use any connection you gain from these activities to schedule a cup of coffee with someone from that company. Chances are these people may even know someone at one of the places on your Target List and can refer you to a person there.

The goal of making this Target List is not only to give you an idea of the companies that you would be interested in contacting, *but it will also be used in all of your conversations during the ensuing HSE steps of the process.* Showing this list to people during conversations will help them clearly understand the kind of organization you are seeking. Anyway, you couldn't ask for a better "conversation starter!"

TAKE AWAY

The end result of this unit is a list of companies and people that you would like to talk with for the benefit of research—NOT to land a job, but to discover the unique needs of businesses and to explore the possibilities on how you can solve their problems.

What will you do now at 8:00 a.m. tomorrow morning?

Chapter 17

UNIT RECAP: Research

1. Begin by identifying the types of positions that you have in your Objective Statement. What industries use those types of positions (find their common SIC code)? What job titles fit the type of work that you have defined? What are the common responsibilities of a person with that type of job (look at job postings across the country for that type of job and find common words or requirements that keep showing up in the postings)? What different names are used for this type of job in various industries?

2. Use your local library to research which organizations exist within a 30-mile radius of your desired location that have the SIC codes you have identified as possibilities. You will be shocked at the number of organizations that you have not been aware of previous to this research. Research sites like Hoovers or Reference USA are very helpful, but they are paid sites that the library or local college or university might have access to for free. Books like your state's manufacturing and service guides will be available and use the same SIC code system.

3. Create a profile of the type of organization that fits what you are looking for in the next position you hold. Consider variables like number of employees, for-profit/non-profit, privately/publicly held, established or newer company, industry, service, or manufacturing based, etc. Creating and sticking to this profile will not only make you aware of organizations that you didn't know existed, but it will also ensure you are only focusing on organizations that would be a good fit for you. Remember, if you don't know where you are going, any road will get you there.

4. Cross your organizational profile with the organizations that you become aware of by doing the research. Then create a list of target companies. These are not necessarily ones you want to work for; they are resources that you would like to learn more about using the *HSE* method.

5. After creating your Target List of companies, continue your research on each of these organizations to become aware of their employees, recent news and events that involve the company, products or services, and competitors. Remember, this information will help you identify other organizations that would value your skills and experience.

6. Share your Target List with people on your 1000/1000 List and on your ABC List. Make them aware that you are researching these organizations and at some point would appreciate their help connecting with someone there or with a person who has ties to that company.

7. Evaluate the list of target companies. Read their websites and news stories. What common words or themes do they use in their value or mission statements? What common problems or opportunities do they share? Are those ideas reflected in your skill set?

8. Use your ABC List and 1000/1000 List. Make sure to create this list one day and then revisit it a couple days later to ensure that other people WILLING to help you make the list (you may not think of everyone in one list-making session). Keep your ABC List close to your phone or e-mail so you can add to it as you go through this process.

9. Cross reference your ABC List and 1000/1000 list against your Target List of organizations. Are there any commonalities?

10. The goal is research through discussions with people in the job type or industry you have targeted. What problems do they face and how would your skill set solve them?

Chapter 18
MARKETING (YOU)

**The *Human Search Engine*
INSTRUCTIONAL PROCESS STEP 6:**

Networking the *Human Search Engine* way.

The research you just concluded is now in place as the cornerstone of a new life skill, and it is ready to use with the final phase of the *Human Search Engine* process: Marketing You.

Each time I begin to speak at a seminar, teach a class, or work with an individual client or student, the conversation eventually turns to networking. and the gist of the dialogue never fails to surprise me. Almost without fail, the moment "networking" comes up, I see a chorus line of eyes slightly roll back in heads. I hear these people say that everyone knows they are looking for a job. I congratulate them, with a hint of sarcasm.

I tell them that their efforts thus far aren't so much networking as they are about being a beggar on a street corner, holding a cup. It is at this moment that I can begin to reshape the strategies of jobseekers for the rest of their life.

To begin, let's discuss a common misconception about what *Human Search Engine* networking is and what it is not. Remember, we have already discussed on numerous occasions in this book how the average person finds virtually everything of value through some sort of networking already. so how can this be much different? The only difference between "everyday" networking and *HSE* networking is now the focus is on your career and your future, making this process tailored and scripted to meeting those very objectives. Oh, and there is nothing random about *HSE* networking.

Human Search Engine networking is NOT:
- Telling your friends that you are looking for a job and to let you know if they hear of anything.
- Randomly "getting in front of" important or influential people so they can hire you.
- Enlisting every recruiter in a 30-mile radius.

- Having random conversations with anyone and then hoping that they "put a good word in for you."
- Dropping off your resume to anyone willing to accept it and then waiting for them to call.

Human Search Engine networking IS:
- A research project. After defining who you are, your first goal is to execute a job search "research project" before looking for a new position.
- Planning and executing a string of logical conversations that progress in an orderly direction toward solving the two biggest problems of job search: 1) No one knows you exist, and 2) You are currently unaware of at least 85% of the organizations that could hire you now.
- All about conversing with the right people who are WILLING to help you on your search, while teaching them how to get you to people who are then ABLE to help you on your search.
- A process that is logical, sequential, experiential, and terminal.
- The only way to get hired by smart organizations today. The *HSE* process is free (for the organization looking to hire its next great employee), fast, requires little work, and provides qualified and credible candidates without a huge hiring process.

Networking the wrong way can hurt your job search

Now, let's explore some more common misconceptions about the value of networking and describe why networking the wrong way (not the *HSE* way) can actually *hurt your job search efforts.*

There are no straight lines in networking. It is important to understand that by the time jobseekers come to one of my seminars or workshops, almost of all of them have been doing their job search independently for an average of three months. These are intelligent and successful people in their own rite who are likely going to be great hires for some company. So if these people are smart and accomplished, why do they struggle with their job search?

The answer is. the very traits that made them successful in their careers up to this point are now posing tremendous barriers during a job search. The ideas and methodology that got them hired and promoted in the past are now the very things that are keeping them unemployed. Let me explain.

Any structured, successful organization (for-profit, non-profit, public, etc.) highly values efficiency, especially today. A business' goal is to continuously get from one defined point to another within a process in the least amount of time, using the fewest possible resources (often referred to as LEAN in business).

Productivity is the name of the game. Speed and quality output are the measures used to evaluate employees on whether they earn a bonus, are reorganized into another role, or possibly fired. Fewer things are more valued in business than creating a desired end result with the least possible resources at the lowest cost. It's about the bottom line.

We have to stop looking at the "bottom line" in business as something evil. Yes, corruption exists in business like it does in human behavior, and the media make the most out of scrutinizing these organizations until they're blue in the face. We get it: Greed is unhealthy and unethical.

At the same time, we also have an obligation to give benefit of the doubt to accepting that the vast majority of businesses are out to make money for the right reasons. In my world, I deal with business people every day, including owners and managers, and 99% of them are good people. They want to contribute to their local economy, donate to charities, and more importantly, give employees many opportunities for a better quality of life.

So, what is our role in this equation as jobseekers? In business today, the global economy is pushing competition to levels that companies have never seen before. Businesses are trying to outdo one another in times that necessitate LEAN operations, environmental adaptations, increased government regulations, and worldwide competition for cheap labor. We can cry about it and even try to change it if desired, but I would recommend exerting our energies into being part of the plans that organizations are devising to adapt to a new way of doing of business.

The catch is that in order to manage a process or a negotiation, you have to not only be part of it, but you need to take some control over it. In the case of networking your way into a joyful career the *HSE* way, you have to *control the conversation during networking opportunities*. Negotiating pricing with a vendor is easy if you have control over whether or not a purchase will be made. In that case, you control the conversation.

In networking the conventional way during a job search, however, how often have you had control over the conversation? Heck, you don't even have control over whether someone will talk to you at all! This is why *HSE* networking is so important to learn.

> *In networking the conventional way during a job search, however, how often have you had control over the conversation? Heck, you don't even have control over whether someone will talk to you at all! This is why HSE networking is so important to learn.*

You were once important (and you will be again). That's the good news.

Remember, networking is not about getting in front of the most people; it's about getting in front of the right people who need you to solve their problems.

It's imperative to embrace that no matter how much authority or power you wielded in previous jobs, you are now dependent on the help of others in your job search. You don't have control over anything other than your actions to market yourself to people and organizations that have the problems you can uniquely solve. This can be a very tough pill to swallow for people. especially if they really carried some clout in their last job or in previous careers. I even have a name for this type of jobseeker: a PIP, or "Previously Important Person."

PIPs often withdraw from the idea that they need help from anybody. They will typically infer the saying, "Don't you know who I am?" just by their attitude or conversations. I often respond accordingly by asking, "You mean, don't I know who you were?" This is a humbling moment for even the most successful PIP.

I don't say it to be mean, but it does serve as a gentle slap in the face. It's a realization for a PIP that his/her search will be based on who they are. not on who they were. It is a moment when they further realize their lack of success in job search is due to going at it alone with visions of previous grandeur guiding the now clouded effort. They also slowly begin to recall the first precursor of the *HSE* job search: **Be humble, be sincere, and ask for help.**

Your job search is manageable just like other projects you have done in the past

A key element in my ability to change the path of a person's job search focuses on making them understand that this project is not unlike a dozen other projects they've already done in their business life. Most jobseekers have had experience during their career in taking something from concept to completion. from idea to reality. The tasks they've seen through were usually given to them by their supervisor as a project to be completed in a certain period of time.

Let's suppose for a moment that you were working as a salesperson in charge of selling what you believe is the world's best hammer. This hammer that you are in charge of promoting is truly unique and unlike any hammer that people had ever seen before. The hammer's special traits appear to be useful to a number of different industries and in a dozen different ways for each of those industries.

You are certain that if you could only get this hammer in front of people who would value its unique qualities, they would buy it and recommend the product to every organization in the industry. How in the world do you get the word out about this hammer, under the assumption that advertising and other promotional tactics are likely out of your control (there we go again—"out of control") due to budgetary constraints, time restrictions, lack of resources, etc.

You really have two problems in determining how to promote this amazing hammer:

- Even though this hammer appears on the surface to look like every other hammer on the market, how do you get people to see how special it really is? Can you articulate what is unique and beneficial about this particular hammer?
- How do you determine which people and industries value the unique capabilities of this hammer?

If these two questions were effectively addressed, you could sell a lot of hammers! The process of hitting the mark on these two questions is exactly what the *HSE* job search process is all about. It should come as no surprise, that in this case, YOU are the unique and special hammer. That's right, we are going to do this research and promote you the same way that people have promoted tools and cans of tomato soup for 100 years. the process just hasn't been recognized and adopted by the 'people business' as a whole.

Here's a way to summarize the hammer example as if it related to you in your current job search situation. In these steps, the hammer is "you."

- Identify the unique characteristics of the hammer
- Identify who values those unique characteristics
- Uncover new markets of hammer buyers that are not obvious to the average salesperson because he or she is not using an *HSE* process
- Actively promote to those new markets that need this special hammer

More and more companies are starting to use the *HSE* to hire their talent because they are finding immediate value. It's wise to be ready for any opportunity at the front of the line to present your unique characteristics to these smart companies.

Now we're inching closer to solving those two problems that ever jobseeker has. no one knows you exist, and you're unaware of 85% of organizations that would value your skills.

If you solve these two problems, a job is not far away.

The real purpose of networking

Why do people struggle so much with the idea of networking during their job search? After working with thousands of jobseekers, I believe I finally have an answer. In career search, most people have been taught about networking as a tool to beg for a job. That doesn't work. It didn't work in the past and especially considering the tight job market today, it won't work now either.

Whether it's during my job search sessions or working one-on-one with clients, the responses I hear about networking are very predictable and generally evolve around:

- I'm already doing that, but it hasn't worked so far.
- I want to make real progress with my job search, not spend my time having random conversations with strangers.
- I don't really know any important people that can get me a job.
- I have no desire to cold call on a dozen businesses and try to get them to interview me.

These responses are all too revealing. You see, in job search it's "what we think we know" that gets us into the most trouble. Most jobseekers have preconceived notions about:

- The economy and that jobs don't exist because it is what the media tell us
- Educational degrees that sound the coolest will get me hired
- The vitality of large corporations (mostly manufacturers) is not stable because that's what the media tell us
- Smaller companies don't pay anything
- You have to know someone or forget about finding a good job
- Work is just a way to pass time and earn a paycheck
- What worked in our last job search will automatically work again

The hardest part of a job search might be admitting that what we "know" might not be true. If you're going at your next career the *HSE* way, let's admit:

- It's not always society's fault when our efforts don't work
- Sometimes we need help during a job search
- Asking the right people to help us and how to ask them is a learned skill
- We really are unaware of 85% of the organizations that could hire us
- Our ego could be getting in the way
- There is an entirely different way to search for a job, but businesses use this process everyday to launch new products and services.

It only goes to reason that if a person has climbed the corporate ladder through sheer will and determination on his/her own part, the act of asking for help during a job search will be very hard. Harder yet is knowing you have been out of work for three, six, or nine months or even a year, and that the world seems to be spinning along just fine without you.

Willing vs. Able: A Short Story

Imagine for a moment that I asked you to go out and network in order to get a $10,000 loan for a really great business idea. If you are like most people, your mind will go to two places almost simultaneously.

- "I don't know anybody who has that type of money to loan out."
- "Who is going to trust me enough to lend me that kind of money even if they have it."

Each of these questions represents your actual thoughts of: Question #1. Who is WILLING to help you find the money?. and Question #2. Who is actually ABLE to lend you that type of money?

The vast majority of people would begin to focus on the second question, "Who is actually ABLE to lend you that type of money?" Our business philosophy tells us that the most efficient way to get this loan is to talk to people that you reasonably believe would have that type of money to lend. You might make lists of successful people, business owners, bankers, people you read about who got inheritances, etc. I mean, talking to people who don't have that much money to lend is just a waste of time; they are not **ABLE** to lend you that amount of money. Right?

Our networking sense is that we should try to "cozy up" to rich people or present them with a brilliant business plan. We might begin to put together slide shows or dazzling sales pitches to influence them. Even though these people don't know us, we are sure that this proposition has enough merit that they will believe in our idea enough to make a worthwhile investment.

With our sales presentations, slide shows, value propositions, and elevator introductions firmly in-hand, we set out to visit with the first rich person we can find. Confidently, we greet this total stranger, and then we proceed right into conveying our practiced sales pitch. We entice them for the first 10 seconds with a scripted introduction. The rich person listens intently for the first 10 seconds (all while wondering. who are you and why are you here?) until you get to the part of your presentation asking them to loan you $10,000.

With a quizzical look, the person quickly says he/she is not interested. It even appeared for a split second the person found your proposition attractive. You wonder is disbelief, "How can this be possible?" I have a great message, and they are ABLE to lend me the money. what could have gone wrong?

Your keen business sense tells you to not stop with the first no, and so you press on to the next affluent person on the list. In a desperate effort to make this interaction better than the last one, you change up your slide show and a few words in the introduction. With confidence, you're lucky enough to land another meeting with this busy, successful person (by the way, securing a meeting is half the battle in the approach being discussed right now—something also to keep in mind as *HSE* teaches how to go about it the right way). You do your sales pitch all over again. While the person with money listens for a short period of time, once again he/she refuses and closes the door on the opportunity.

For the next week, you spend 40 hours making presentations to these strangers on your list and make no progress. You begin to question the value of your business proposal. Is it really as good as you thought it was? You question your presentation skills and value in the world. By the end of the week you begin to conclude that "times are tough" and now is just not the right time for anyone to invest. In other words, you say to yourself, "See, there are no jobs out there (remember our analysis of "out there") because that's what the newspapers are telling."

After your hard week you decide to have a beer with your best friend from high school. You guys have been friends forever and would do anything for one other. You have been through good times and bad and have even helped each other out of tough jams. Some people even call you "twins from different mothers" because you see the world in the same way. you guys are tight.

Your best friend asks, "Hey, can you spring for the beers tonight? I don't have a penny to my name until payday next week." You quickly remember that your buddy is not really good with money and spends it as fast as he earns it. He is a great guy, but there is no way in the world that he would be ABLE to lend you the money you need. The two of you start discussing your past week, and you share with your friend how the meetings went concerning your business idea.

You describe to your broke friend that you just don't understand why you're not making any progress. You have a great business idea and these people clearly are ABLE to lend you the money. it has been so frustrating. You say out loud, "Anyone who knows me understands that I would never ask for a loan unless the idea was solid." You also forget that none of the people you met with even know you.

Your penniless friend asks, "Well, I know you. Why didn't you ever come to me with this idea?" Sheepishly, you tell him that you know he doesn't have that type of money. You further disclose that while the two of you would do anything for each other, you didn't want to put him on the spot because you knew his financial situation. He wouldn't be ABLE to lend you the money.

"What's wrong with you?" he shouts back at you. "Of course I don't have that type of money, but my uncle is part of an angel investing group and they look at deals much bigger than this every day!" You reply, "You would be WILLING to introduce me to your uncle?" "Don't be silly," he responds. "We are very close and he has always given me great advice. He has even told me that if I ever ran across a good idea worth investing in that I should tell him about it right away. Besides, you are my best friend in the world. I may not have the money, but I am WILLING to put my reputation on the line in front of my uncle."

A week later you are in front of your friend's uncle making your sales pitch. The uncle seems interested, but a little unsure about your idea. Your friend steps up and tells him about your personal and professional friendship. He even informs him about the great business ideas you've come up with in the past. His uncle agrees to let you present in front of his angel investor group.

The big day arrives and you are ready to present in front of this group of successful investors. now these people are definitely ABLE to lend you the money! You are confident of your success right until you enter the boardroom. To your complete horror, six of the people sitting on the angel investor group are the strangers that you presented to during your first week of door knocking! Your heart sinks. They have already turned me down face to face and now I'm about to be shot down again! As you begin presenting your great idea you feel doomed.

"Aren't you that young man who knocked on my door a few weeks ago?" one of them asks. "Yes sir, I am," you reply. "Didn't I tell you then that I wasn't in favor of your idea?" the same man asks. "I don't know you. How do I know that you really have credible ideas worth investing in?"

Before a word leaves your mouth, your friend's uncle steps in. "My nephew has known this young man his whole life. He says he's had dozens of great business ideas over the years that have been funded and done well; I say we hear him out."

Ironically, 90 minutes later you are being patted on the back by some of the same people who knocked down your idea just a week or two earlier. You stand stunned in disbelief while holding a $10,000 check in your hand. How could this be? I had the same idea for the same amount of money that involved some of the same people. What happened?

Your friend's uncle takes you aside to congratulate you. You ask him that very same question, "What changed?" With a wry smile the uncle replies, "You made the first and biggest mistake last week. You focused on people that were ABLE to help you on your project, but they were not WILLING to help you. My nephew, on the other hand, was extremely WILLING to help you and he vouched for you as a genuine person with sound business ideas."

The uncle continues, "To be honest with you, had you knocked on my door a week ago I would have said no to your proposal as well. I didn't trust you when I agreed to help you; I trust my nephew and his judgment of you. I knew full well that he was putting his personal and professional reputation on the line when he brought you to me. If you were good enough for him to trust, you were good enough for me."

Willing and Able come together in HSE networking

As you might guess by now after reading the story, the *HSE* way of networking focuses 95% of our time interacting with people who are WILLING to help you. Those are the people who will get you in front of others who are ABLE to help you.

The traditional way of jumping right to people who are ABLE to help you may be somewhat efficient on the surface, but it is not effective in the long run. It's particularly ineffective in today's business climate when so much technology is diluting the relational side of conducting business anyway (social media, texting, email, etc.). Moreover, is it really that efficient anyway when you have to redo your plan, while wasting all of that time scheduling appointments with very busy people in the first place?

Remember, we are networking by creating business relationships with people. When is the last time that you achieved a meaningful relationship with anyone by forcing efficiency ("I'd like you to be my friend and you have 20 seconds to decide".)? All meaningful relationships in your life, business or personal, have been formed by making a connection with the person.

TAKE AWAY:

Networking is nothing more than collecting business cards unless you do it with a plan and a purpose the *HSE* way. Remember, be humble, be sincere, and ask for help. When going to people who are ABLE to help you, it will only work when you have a connection to these individuals or when you have something to offer them in return.

With *HSE*, you control your ability to connect with people and enable them decide to help you, all while coming across as *the solution* to their problems. Everything we do from this point in this process is to guide people who are WILLING to help us get to individuals who are ABLE to help us.

Chapter 19

MARKETING (YOU)

The *Human Search Engine* INSTRUCTIONAL PROCESS STEP 7:

You must become interesting before you become important

We just concluded an important learning objective in that networking vs. *Human Search Engine* networking is a very significant distinction. In addition, remember too from the previous chapter that every jobseeker has two problems he or she must solve in order to land a rewarding job:

- Nobody knows you exist—a company can't hire you until it knows you exist.
- You are currently unaware of at least 85% of the organizations that could use you.

Again, the *Human Search Engine* was designed to solve these two problems!

Most job search books spend a great deal of time recommending that you invest your money in career counseling firms and how to artfully present your achievements through fancy resumes, cover letters, and portfolios. I totally disagree! Why? Well, for starters, let's look at every new personal relationship that you have formed in your life for clues.

One of the things about the *HSE* process that is so important is that what I am teaching you is already a part of your daily life. I encourage my students to challenge every one of my philosophies against how things have worked in their own lives. I want to make sure that people trying to use the *HSE* method know that this is no infomercial, new age, miracle-inducing system. People are smart enough to know that anyone who promotes weight loss without diet and exercise as the keys is pulling your leg. Lose weight while you sleep. REALLY? The old saying goes that if something is too good to be true, it probably is.

That's why this is so different. *HSE* teaches you to do things you already do and have done, use the people experience you have from your own life and put them into a process-oriented project plan that leads you to a predictable result.

Look at the world around you. How do products and services get sold? How do you decide to buy things and what influences your decisions? After just a few moments of watching TV or being online, the answer comes to you very quickly. marketing.

Unmistakable jingles and taglines ("You're in good hands with.") create lasting messages. It is clear that nothing in this country is bought or sold without a planned and sustained marketing effort. If marketing is a good strategy for billion dollar international companies, I'm pretty sure it's relevant for jobseekers as well.

In order to market any product (in this case, your skills and abilities) we need to have a story to tell. Commercials sell products because their message connects with people. Our *HSE* marketing effort will be no different.

Relationships of any kind form slowly over time and begin with a simple introduction and finding of common interests. Our job search marketing will follow those same rules and consist of three levels of conversation as we introduce ourselves to people who don't currently know us: **1) the Tagline, 2) the Focus Statement, and 3) the 60-Second Introduction.**

These three messages will carry us from the initial introduction (Tagline) to creation of interest in a conversation (Focus Statement) all the way through describing of our technical skills and job search target (60-Second Introduction). It just seems to make sense to design our introduction and generation of interest with someone the same way that you have done it in your personal life 500 or more times.

Your Tagline

Taglines are not new, and frankly, we are surrounded by them all day long. These short 5-10 word phrases are designed to catch someone's attention, create interest, and invite questions. Are they important? To some degree, Presidents of the United States are elected largely in part due to taglines or sound bites over the evening news (some memorable phrases include "It's the economy, stupid," "Are you better off today than you were four years ago," and "We need hope and change," to name a few). I guess if the most powerful person in the world relies on them—maybe you should too.

One of the ways that you will gain the attention of key players in your *HSE* job search is to create a tagline that resembles some sort of **oxymoron** (Exs: jumbo shrimp, peace through aggression) or **non-sequitur statement** (a statement where one of the items just doesn't seem to belong with the others, like pickles and ice cream). The goal of these statements is to make someone a little perplexed, yet anxious to learn more.

Consider these concepts to be like a catchy hook before giving a presentation or writing a persuasive article. I like to think an effective tagline will make a person spin around like a German shepherd hearing a high-pitched whistle. Our goal is first to get attention and then invite questions from that person because they want to learn more.

Along the same lines as the previous chapter's theme, "You can't push your way into any organization; you have to be invited". is the ability to get people to ask questions after delivering our tagline. This serves as an "invitation" to continue the conversation. Pushing your way into any new relationship is not a good idea. Jobseekers need to stop pushing their way into organizations.

An example of an effective Tagline is the one that I have used for years as a career counselor, "A plan to take the fear out of job search." How does this fit the criteria explained above? First, the word fear instantly catches someone's attention. Anyone who has ever been on a job search knows the fear that I am referring to. It's about the fear of how long the money will last or the fear of being judged by someone. real distresses to jobseekers.

The non-sequitur in my Tagline is the combination of the words "plan" and "job search" used together in the same sentence. For most people without an advanced understanding of job search, they cannot conceive the idea that you have enough control over your search for it to constitute being a plan. Even if someone could comprehend this idea, how would he or she know it's a useful plan and even how to execute it?

Initial reactions to my Tagline almost always make people say, "Tell them more about that" or something of that nature. That's the whole goal, isn't it? The final result of what started as your Tagline could be an extension of immediate dialogue or a face-to-face, one-hour informal meeting or actual interview! The beginning point, however, on the path to that final destination of meeting personally is an initial connection that gets them to want to learn more.

Here are some other samples of good Taglines:

- Creating a brand without saying a word (for marketing professionals)
- The pain-free dentist
- An IT professional who speaks English
- An attorney who stays out of court
- An administrative professional who can create order out of chaos

Now, write your own Tagline and test it on a few people who you know. Does it get them to ask questions? Remember, the Tagline doesn't tell the whole story; it simply gets other people interested enough in your greeting to ask you for more information. At this time, let's explore how to use a Tagline in order to optimize its potential.

When you meet someone new and the person asks what you do for a living, give them your Tagline. I understand that type of question (What you do for a living?) can be hard to answer for someone who is unemployed. Practice it for a while as a ready response. Then, again try your Tagline on a few people who you know personally (WILLING), but who you don't know on a professional basis (UNABLE).

See how they react. You may have to adjust your response a bit along the way based on certain personalities—perhaps modify your nonverbal communication or tone when stating the Tagline. Don't be cute with your Tagline though. puns are fine, but don't go overboard. The only good Tagline is the one that gets people to ask, "What do you mean by that?" That question is an open invitation to an important business conversation. Remember, you can't push your way into a conversation—you have to be invited.

> The only good Tagline is the one that gets people to ask, "What do you mean by that?" That question is an open invitation to an important business conversation. Remember, you can't push your way into a conversation—you have to be invited.

Finally, start using your Tagline as a branding statement during job search. List it on your job search business cards (yes, you need business cards for your job search—how will people know how to contact you?) and say it often at networking events and job fairs. Businesses spend billions being known by only a few words. let's follow their lead.

Your Focus Statement

There is an old saying: "Nobody cares how much you know until they know how much you care." Think about that for a moment. We've all been taught or influenced to conduct a job search by dazzling people with our technical and people skills, and there is a time for that (coming next in the 60-Second Introduction). Again, think of every new relationship (personal or business) that you have formed in your life. After you say hello to a person (your Tagline), what is the next thing that the two of you do? If you are like most people, the next thing you do is find common ground to discuss. Often you will talk about the weather, an event, a sports contest, a TV show, work, etc.

Our goal is to choreograph the first moments of every conversation that we engage in with a new person during the *HSE* search. We know that there will be an awkward silence about 15 seconds into the conversation (like there has been in your conversations with every new person you've met and will meet). This is where your Focus Statement comes in.

The goal of the Focus Statement is easy to understand, but very hard for some people to grasp because it contains no work history, no achievements, no education, and no tangible results. This runs contrary to how most people theoretically introduce themselves, hence the reason they struggle with the concept. We have been taught (or heard nothing else but) since our first job search to impress people with our accomplishments so they kneel down and roll out the red carpet for us.

So, let's look at a typical conversation with any new person who you will meet moving forward. You introduce yourself and shortly engage in a discussion about what both of you do for a living (wow, that Tagline could sure come in handy here). After you nod in acknowledgement of that information, the silence drives you to try another mutual topic of interest. You will talk about where you live, where you grew up, where you went to school. all in a very emotionless exchange of facts that the other person can't really expound on. Then you hit on something that you both feel strongly about and the conversation changes immediately. It may be politics, sports, volunteering, a local referendum, etc.,. anything where a shared passion comes into play.

> **We have been taught (or heard nothing else but) since our first job search to impress people with our accomplishments so they kneel down and roll out the red carpet for us.**

The above self-examination of any conversational experience serves as a reminder that no one creates a meaningful relationship in minutes, especially when trying to impress another person (which was not the case above, but see how hard it was to establish a relationship without even trying to impress?). If you aim to impress, the other person will quickly ask where the restroom is or excuse him or herself to grab a coffee—only not to return. If the two of you don't find some common ground where you share passion on a topic, the conversation goes south pretty quickly and then straight to the exits.

If that is true with the hundreds of people you have met in your own life, how can it possibly not be true in networking for a job? Remember, "Nobody cares how much you know until they know how much you care." No young man looking to introduce himself to a young lady starts the conversation with his achievements, education, or technical description of who they are. Can you imagine that conversation:

"Hi my name's Ben and I'm six foot one inches tall and weigh 195 pounds. I'm a graduate of a prestigious university and have very good teeth. I make $50,000 a year as an accountant, but my parents have a lot of money and I stand to inherit it someday. Would you like to go out with me?"

Wow. Ask any young lady to read that last paragraph and then ask her what she thinks of that type of intro (with exceptions, of course—it's rather humorous, but I know you see the point). You don't use that kind of introduction in your own life, so how can you believe that it will work in networking for job search. Remember, we are talking about networking here. not the conversation with a hiring manager for an open position. With a hiring manager in an interview, your achievements are certainly going to be part of the conversation, but we are meeting new people in this context.

You have to become interesting before you can become important.

The passion you need in that conversation is in your Focus Statement

Focus Statements are about passion for the work you do. That's it! When we get to the next part of your introduction (the 60-Second Intro), I promise you will get every chance to unveil all of your achievements, skills, and philosophies. For now, let's just focus on letting people know why you decided to become a dentist instead of a circus clown. What is it about being an engineer that makes you leap out of bed every day? Is there something from your childhood experiences that made you focus on becoming a teacher since the age of 10? Did someone impact your life in a really positive way, and now you want to do the same kind of work that this person did because of that influence?

There is usually some seminal moment when you decided to do the kind of work that you do. Perhaps your father was an accountant, and you saw that it provided a good, steady life for his family. Furthermore, his career allowed your mom to stay home with you (or maybe your mom was the accountant and dad stayed home). Did a police officer or firefighter influence your life in a positive way and you became drawn to one of these professions? Where you naturally mechanically curious as a child and drove your parents crazy tearing things apart because you just had to know how they worked? Did a doctor or nurse play a critical role in your family's life? Was there a teacher who influenced you early in your educational career? Was there a TV show that piqued your interest in doing the work you do now? Have you always had an innate desire to help people?

In a nutshell, the *HSE* Focus Statement is about your passion and drive to do the type of work that you seek in your next position. It is the brief, 20-30 second story that you share with someone when discussing your job search. Subsequently, the Focus Statement gives this person an idea of your industry of interest. Make no mistake about it. people will only refer you to their personal and professional acquaintances if they are convinced that your integrity and passion for doing this work is evident in everything that you do.

Remember, people are putting their reputation on the line every time a referral is done in the credible networking process known as the *Human Search Engine*. So why is passion for your work so important in the first minute when you meet someone? What does being passionate about your work guarantee this other person?

I must answer the two preceding questions with a question to provoke some important thought here. What do we know for sure about passionate people in our lives? Think for a second about the three or four people in your life who you know are truly passionate about what they do. Picture them in your mind. what do they look like? What do they sound like? How hard do they work to improve themselves for the greater good of their work and the people around them?

The point here is what makes a "good employee?" When there are six inches of newly-fallen snow on the ground, what efforts do these people make to get to work that day? **If you were to refer them to one of your personal or professional friends, how sure are you that they will represent you well?** That's the question that matters here in our discussion about whether people will refer you to others during your search.

Remember: Be humble, be sincere, and ask for help. Your passion about whatever work you do is the best way to exemplify "being sincere" on a moment-by-moment basis. You should light up when you give your Focus Statement. It should be apparent to everyone around you that this topic and this work excites you. *When you deliver your Focus Statement, you should have a look on your face like "a five-year old talking about Santa Claus on Christmas Eve!"*

Focus Statement Parameters and Sample

Here are the parameters of your Focus Statement:

- It should only last 20-30 seconds
- It should be in a story format that "paints a picture"
- You should deliver it with genuine passion (without going overboard, of course)
- Your experiences that led you to your line of work must resonate clearly as a conclusion

As a point of reference, here is my Focus Statement when I first meet people who wonder why I teach job search for a living:

"When it comes to job search, I have made every mistake a person can make. I've chosen a career based on a TV show, run scared to an industry that I would never have chosen for myself, spent 20 years in leadership positions in an industry I couldn't have cared less about, chased money, worked for incompetent and evil bosses, and then out of desperation and lucky timing, learned an incredible new way to look for a job that made perfect sense. but I had never heard of it. My goal in teaching this job search process is to let people learn from my mistakes and empower them to take control of their lives."

Do you have a picture in your mind right now? Do you have questions for me? Does my passion for this work make sense to you? Are you interested in learning more?

Good Focus Statements pull people into a conversation and cause them to invite you further in. From there, the dialogue generates further interest. **You have become interesting before you became important.**

Now, write your Focus Statement. Dig deep and forget about impressing people. Focus on engaging them. Test it on people who you know personally, but not professionally. If it draws them into the conversation, you now have their attention enough to start talking about your qualifications, experiences, and achievements. enter your **60-Second Introduction.**

Your 60-Second Introduction

This is the point when most *HSE* jobseekers tuck away their desire to proclaim, "I need to tell people how great I am that they will be so impressed to hire me!" If that's truly the case, you have been with me every step of the way throughout the process. It is a validation that you have learned one HUGE lesson.

You realize now that you're getting closer to graduating from the *Human Search Engine* in the form of landing a job that you look forward to doing each day. Let's continue a little bit longer to reach that pinnacle point for you in your life.

While you will definitely be using some of your skills and accomplishments as part of your introduction, you will be melding those elements with a continued attempt to connect with the person who you are speaking with.

Remember our saying, "You can't push your way into any organization or relationship. you have to be invited." The 60-Second Introduction is your chance to build credibility with a person while maintaining interest in your story.

In the *HSE* world, there are five parts to a 60-Second Introduction:

1. Restate your name and give people a way to remember it (My name is Chris Czarnik—that's 'czar' like Czar of Russia and 'nik' like Nicolas).

2. Describe what you are looking for in your next position in terms of duties, level, responsibilities, and industry (the goal here is to paint a picture of where someone has seen that type of job before so you are discussing the same type of job). Don't just use a job title. Remember, there are managers of local convenience stores (with all due respect) and there are managers of divisions of multi-national organizations.

3. Provide a brief work history (20 seconds or less and make sure you demonstrate a logical transition from your previous positions to the job you are looking to land next).

4. Describe an achievement that you are proud of and/or brought value to an organization (make sure this accomplishment is measurable and demonstrates the skills you are claiming to possess).

5. Offer a work-related tidbit that helps set the stage for the small talk that inevitably ensues after your introduction is complete (We know that the two of you will be searching for something to discuss after you stop talking. Instead of hoping that the topic will show you in a positive light, let's make sure it does by "priming the pump.").

A sample 60-Second Introduction:

1. "Hi, my name is Chris Czarnik—that's Czar like Czar of Russia and Nik like Nicolas."

2. "What I'm looking for in my next position is an opportunity to speak in front of large audiences in a high school or college setting on the topics of career choices and job search. This would a paid presenter position in an independent consultant role. The opportunity would occur on any given campus once or twice a year, and would entail about one-to-three hour job search workshops to better prepare students for their job search after graduation. I would be supporting the ongoing efforts of the school's career center."

3. "My work experience includes more than 20 years of leadership roles, including the military and industry with a heavy concentration on HR and hiring manager responsibilities. For the past decade, I have been teaching professional job search to more than 300 individual executive clients while working for a national career search firm. Four years ago, I started my own company and have been traveling the Midwest speaking at high schools, colleges, and universities on the topics of career choice and job search."

4. "I am proud to say that in 2005 I was recognized as an outstanding career advisor for a national career search firm, and in 2008 was contracted by the University of Wisconsin-Madison, a school of more than 45,000 students to write the career search curriculum for a division of the college. I now teach that job search curriculum to the athletic department as a guest instructor several times a semester."

5. "One of the most interesting things about working with the university's athletic department is that the football and basketball players who you watch on ESPN on Saturday are in my classroom on Tuesday."

Think of the last part. number 5—the interesting work-related tidbit of information. What questions do you think surface after I finish delivering that statement? They run the gamut. "Are the players really that strong (or fast)?" "How do they get their homework done with all that traveling?" "Are athletes smart?"

Regardless of what questions the person asks, we will be talking about one of the things that I am most proud of in my career. working at UW-Madison, the fifth largest research university in the United States. It is virtually impossible for the first five minutes of the conversation to be dull or uninteresting, and how long does it take for a person to decide if he or she will connect with someone new? You guessed it. less than five minutes, if not a matter of seconds.

Here's a good old-fashioned assignment for you:

Revise or write your Tagline, Focus Statement, and 60-Second Introduction. Try it first on people who you know really well. See if they think it is a good reflection of who you really are. You may need to revise these conversational pieces several times along the *HSE* journey as you gain feedback from others.

> *It is virtually impossible for the first five minutes of the conversation to be dull or uninteresting, and how long does it take for a person to decide if he or she will connect with someone new? You guessed it–less than five minutes, if not a matter of seconds.*

After you get these three pieces nailed down, then test them on people who you know professionally—in other words, folks who have a good feel for your skill set. These will be people who you have worked with in the past. Do they think it's an accurate professional representation of you as well? Does it make them want to ask questions?

How will you know when you've got it right? Well, in the immortal words of my very smart wife Carlene. you'll just know. When you get the intended reactions and questions. you'll just know. When you deliver it with confidence and vigor. you'll just know. When people are anxious to learn more about you. you'll just know. Keep refining it and colleting feedback from others who want to help you. When will you be ready for the next step, which is doing informational interviews and networking meetings? You guessed it. you'll just know.

Go write it. Go test it. Start easy, start close to home, but start today!

TAKE AWAY:

Develop a Tagline, a Focus Statement, and a 60-Second Introduction. In doing so, you will be ready for a curtain call performance in front of others who are well positioned to help you advance the *HSE* process even closer to landing a great career! Only something "good" in your life will come from this experience. Make it happen, be open to tweaking these three conversational pieces along the way, and learn how to really take control of your life!

Chapter 20

MARKETING (YOU)

The *Human Search Engine* INSTRUCTIONAL PROCESS STEP 8:

Preparing You for Front and Center Conversations

Until now, this book has been about sharing insight on why traditional job searches fail, the job search perspective from the hiring or HR manager's side of the desk, and a step-by-step method to preparing and presenting yourself in a well-planned way to land your next career. You've been awakened to your unique personality, background, skills, as well as what it takes to network as a means of meeting specific goals. You might now be asking yourself, "OK Chris, this is all good stuff, but what do I need to do to put the *Human Search Engine* into action to change my outcomes with job search?" Your journey is about to be rewarded.

Once again, remember the theory—the HSE process needs to solve the two biggest problems in job search: 1) Nobody knows you exist, and 2) You are currently unaware of 85% of the organizations that could hire you. In simple terms, you lack two things: information and exposure. We are going to fix both of those issues by creating opportunities to be in front of people. That is why you have been sending all of those cover letters and resumes, right? The goal of sending all of these documents was to get an opportunity to have face-to-face conversations in your industry of interest, wasn't it?

> *In simple terms, you lack two things: information and exposure. The HSE process is all about creating these face-to-face opportunities outside of the normal hiring process. That's right, if done correctly, your search will avoid the HR department of an organization all together until someone from inside the company brings you there for an introduction.*

The *HSE* process is all about creating these face-to-face opportunities outside of the normal hiring process. That's right, if done correctly, your search will avoid the HR department of an organization all together until someone from inside the company brings you there for an introduction.

Remember, you can't push your way into an organization; you have to be invited. Sending resumes and cover letters to a complete stranger at an organization and expecting to end up the choice out of 100 people who applied is a bit of a pipe dream. You are pounding on the door of a party that you're not invited to. Our goal is to have someone from inside the organization open the door of that party for you.

Let's be clear; I have nothing against HR departments. heck, I used to work in one! HR professionals are fine human beings who got into that line of work because they genuinely like people. They are doing the best they to align their own best practices with smart hiring. Until organizations change their mindset and undergoes a complete paradigm shift in hiring, HR professionals must continue to work within a counterproductive system of finding talent. The problem is the system is designed to eliminate you as a candidate for the position. not choose you.

In fact, in a hiring situation where there are 100 applicants for one job, HR's core function is to systematically eliminate 99% of the applicants. In many cases, their first job is not to find the right person; it is to remove who they determine are the wrong people! Intentionally, the process is to find a flaw in your application or resume so they can eliminate you as a candidate.

Again, it's not their fault. Let's walk in their shoes. We are not the ones doing 100 phone screens or 50 first interviews, and even if there are several good candidates, we only have one job available to offer. The awful truth is that in most cases the hiring process is about reaching a manageable number of strong candidates as quickly and systemically as possible. and yes, for the most part, all off of a piece of paper or two.

That's right, you as a candidate spent hours writing and revising your resume and cover letter specifically for that job, applied for the position with great enthusiasm and anticipation, and the first duty of the person who receives it is to find a reason to put it in the "NO" pile. This is not my theory. Again, don't be upset with HR people; question the process.

Before you become more frustrated, ask yourself a different question, "What was the goal of sending the resume and cover letter in the first place?" Did you expect an instant job offer as a result of affixing a stamp on an enclosed envelope containing your resume and cover letter, writing the address on the envelope, and dropping it in a Post Office box on the street corner?

No! You sent in the resume and cover letter hoping someone seeing your information would invite you in for a face-to-face conversation (or bare minimum, a phone interview)! If that is the goal, then the following concept is critical for you to understand.

The HSE method of job search is focused around creating these same face-to-face meetings with hiring managers in a different way—without the power plays and small talk about your favorite color. Think about that for a moment. If I told you there was some secret handshake or magical password that could get you hired. you would be skeptical, as expected. More visible progress with HSE will be your ability to get in front of people who can help you on your search, all while you're in control. This sure beats you being screened out by some computer program because your resume lacked a word or two.

If I've heard it once, I've heard it a thousand times from jobseekers: "If I could only get in front of the people who have the problems they are hiring to solve, I know I could really impress them; the problem is I can't get anyone from that organization to talk to me!" Due to conventional hiring processes that are all about excluding jobseekers from these face-to-face conversations first, great candidates sit at home with a rejection letter while hiring managers ask, "Where's all the talent?" The irony is hiring managers know there is talent somewhere, but how do they find that person? The HSE process is all about making you easy to find for the people who have the problems that your skills will solve.

This connection will not happen accidently. We need to help create the circumstances under which this connection will occur. We will be doing informational interviews and networking meetings so you will show up in front of the person who needs you long before he or she searches for a new hire. We've established you can't push your way into an organization, so we need you to be the answer to their problems by creating opportunities for you to be in the right place at the right time.

Before I close this chapter, I want to cement into your mind the idea that what I am about to teach is something that you have experienced many times in your own life. That's right! The difference is these prior occurrences always happened by accident. We are going to make them happen on purpose.

> More visible progress with HSE will be your ability to get in front of people who can help you on your search, all while you're control. This sure beats you being screened out by some computer program because your resume lacked a word or two.

Almost everyone has had a great restaurant referred to them by a friend or neighbor. "Wow, have you tried the pizza at Luigi's? It's fantastic. you and I like the same type of pizza, and I'm telling you it is great! You've got to go there." What happens next is predictable. You do not scan the ingredients list at Luigi's. You don't do a price comparison between them and all of the other local pizza joints. You go to Luigi's simply based on the recommendation of your fellow pizza-loving friend. Great end result, but did you do anything to make that end result happen? What if you really needed to find a great pizza place but just waited around for someone to recommend one?

In the case of waiting for a recommendation, you don't mention to anyone that you need to find a great pizza place, because you are just sure that if a person knew of one, he or she would initiate this *specific conversation*. You stand there surrounded by pizza aficionados, but nothing is said to you because they have no idea that you need their advice. You become increasingly frustrated with your friends because no one is helping you!

Finally, you get mad at them for not recommending a place to you (even though you never asked) and go visit a random pizza place on your own. Unfortunately, the pizza and the service there are not that good. You conclude that there are no good pizza places in town. because if there were, somebody would have told you about them. I mean, they are your friends after all. At the same time a strange thing is going on. A friend hears that you went to a below-average pizza place and wonders why you chose that restaurant! If asked, he would have been happy to give you advice on another. So, what went wrong here?

This simple story goes a long way to explain why networking often fails, especially when it comes to job search. People randomly apply to organizations that they have never heard of and get nowhere. If they do ask friends for help with their search, typically it is done so like, "If any of you know of any jobs out there, or if you can get me in where you work (the equivalent of asking them to drive you to the pizza place, buy your pizza for you, and clean up your mess), please let me know—thanks." Just like networking for sake of collecting business cards, the above common example of asking for help is basically useless.

We need people's advice, feedback, and guidance, then we will do the rest. We cannot, however, cross our fingers and hope that conversations or advice come out of the blue. We need to initiate the conversation and lead people to giving us guidance that will actually help us. As I say in class all of the time, "People want to help you with your job search but they don't know how. We need to teach them how. Proactive job search means exactly that. we don't wait for things to happen; we make them happen."

The last example I will provide before discussing how to make these conversations happen usually renders the same response in every city that I present in. I was asking my wife (who happens to be my biggest supporter!), Carlene, for a networking example that everyone could relate to. She thought for a moment and said, "Ask the females in the audience how they found their OB-GYN." I didn't understand why at the time that this was such a great question, but the first time I tried it on an audience, the nodding heads told me everything I needed to know.

The decision of which OB-GYN to choose is clearly far too important to ladies than men could ever fathom. The idea of choosing one *without a referral* is met with incredulous looks from virtually every woman in the room. There is no way they would ever throw a dart at the yellow pages and hope an OB-GYN pops out as the one! This decision apparently will never be left to chance! From state-to-state, I hear the same response—women don't wait for a recommendation to find their OB-GYN; they actively solicit advice from other females. The decision would be made no other way.

While I can't speak about the woman-doctor relationship from first-hand knowledge, it's fair to say that where you end up working 2,000 hours a year is a pretty big decision. This is a decision that requires information, advice, and feedback from other people who know more about these companies or industries than you do.

TAKE AWAY:

It's time engage others in your search now that you have a solid grip on who you are, what your skills can do for others, and knowing you need information, advice, and feedback to shape the direction you're heading. Now let's pound that pavement to make some real connections and create those face-to-face opportunities outside of the normal hiring process

Chapter 21
MARKETING (YOU)

The *Human Search Engine* INSTRUCTIONAL PROCESS STEP 9:

Informational Interviews & Networking Meetings

There are two different types of meetings that you will now have as part of the *Human Search Engine* process: Informational Interviews and Networking Meetings. I will compare and contrast them before we discuss how to hold each of these meetings. Frankly, we are at a point now that is really a crowning moment in your job search.

The late legendary hockey coach Herb Brooks said it best to his players as head coach of the 1980 U.S. Olympic 'miracle on ice' gold-medal team just before they hit the ice for that historic game against the Soviet Union: "You have earned the right to be here." Due to your commitment to the *HSE* process, you too have earned the right to be in the position you are in for a better life, and I congratulate you for being at this point in the *HSE* process. You have earned the right to be here.

Informational Interviews: In general terms, you will conduct Informational Interviews with people who "work in the world (industry) that you want to work in next." They have industry-specific knowledge that you will need to know to focus your efforts.

Networking Meetings: People who you will meet with in these meetings may or may not work in your field of expertise (the world that you want to work in next—as noted above), but they flat out "know people." These people may have no direct connection to your industry, but the nature of their work depends on knowing lots of people from all walks of life. Their connections are critical for success. You meet with them so they can introduce you to people who "work in the world you want to work in."

Let's compare and contrast these two types of meetings:

Similarities

Each of these meetings has the following goals:

- To introduce yourself to people who don't know you or to ones who do know you, but don't know how to help you with your job search.
- To gain pertinent information to advance your search efforts. This information might be industry details, names of additional contacts, definition of specific industry problems to be solved, names of organizations inside your desired career that you have never heard of, feedback on your job search presentation, and position descriptions in your field that you did not know existed.
- To be considered and remembered in a positive light by leaving behind a great impression and the idea that you will be an asset to some organization (despite neither of you knowing where that is yet).
- To specifically receive a referral (or two or three) *by name* of someone the other person thinks would be important for you to speak with next to advance your search ("If you were me, who might be the best resource."). By name is a very important component here. If you don't get a direct referral, who do you call tomorrow morning to continue your conversation with?
- To gain specific advice, guidance, and feedback from them (based on your conversation) about how to progress your job search.

Differences

- **Informational Interviews** will focus on industry information that directly relates to your area of expertise. **Networking Meetings** will contain very little conversation about your industry or job type because the person who you are meeting with isn't from that "world."
- The results of **Informational Interviews** will lead you to research the organization or career field to identify specific industry needs or desires you can focus on as a way of creating value as a potential new employee. **Networking Meetings** are focused on people who can get you face-to-face conversations with others to help you with your search through connections.
- **Informational Interviews** will most likely be held with people who are ABLE to help you. **Networking Meetings** will be held with people who are WILLING to help you.
- **Informational Interviews** provide paths to do research and follow up. **Networking Meetings** will seem less direct, but involve teaching people

who are WILLING to help you navigate you to those who are ABLE to help you.

Why do we need two different kinds of meetings in our HSE job search? Both of these meetings answer one of two important questions:

1. **Can I transition into a different type of work or a different industry with my skill set, education, and experience?** In this case (Informational Interview), there are many questions to be answered. You have proven ability in the project management of a small, $5 million manufacturing firm. Could those same skills work for you in a large government organization? You have been a creative marketing design professional your whole career, but now you want to transition into a career in sales. Will a hiring manager see you as a viable candidate? You have been the executive director of a non-profit organization; will decision-makers at for-profit organizations consider you for their positions? The only way to receive insight to these questions is to talk with people who live and work in the type of organization that you want to transition into.

2. **How do I get back into the same job or industry that I was in during my last career?** In this case (Networking Meeting), you have the skills, education, and experience needed to do the job because you demonstrated those traits in your last career. Now all you need is to find similar organizations that have the same types of problems to be solved like the last company you worked for did. The information search will focus on referrals to people who work in those types of organizations.

As you can see, the information that you need to successfully propel your search forward is very different in one transition back to work as opposed to the other. Remember, first and foremost, *HSE* is a research project to find connections and information to lead you to your next position. If we don't clearly define the goal of our search, how do we know what information we need to keep our search moving forward?

Think of the information you need to gather in order to make your transition into a new position like this: "What don't I know about making this transition, and who inside that type of organization could answer that question for me?" Forget entirely about trying to push your way into organizations until you answer this question and others like it *through conversations with people who know the ins and outs because they live in that world.*

Advice, Guidance, and Feedback

It is about this point when I am teaching *HSE* in a classroom that I tend to see a few jobseekers view these meetings as "clever left-hand sells." Some individuals actually think it's time to drop off resumes to these important people instead of experiencing conversations with them. This is an enormous mistake. You need to remember two things about these meetings that you are about to have:

- The people who hold high-level jobs in organizations know exactly what you are trying to accomplish using this method; they have used it most of their professional lives. You see, what I am teaching you is not new. This method of job search has been used by people at upper levels for well over a half of century. Think about it for a moment. Do you really think that the president of a company looks in the Sunday newspaper job ads when he or she is in career transition? Look for yourself if you don't believe me. Visit any job site and look how many "president of company" jobs you find there. Board member jobs? CEO jobs? There are very few. so how do these people find their next position? Networking.

> *You see, what I am teaching you is not new. This method of job search has been used by people at upper levels for well over a half of century. Think about it for a moment. Do you really think that the president of a company looks in the Sunday newspaper job ads when he or she is in career transition?*

- I will promise that the individuals who you meet with through *HSE* can normally read people very well. That's how they got to where they are today. So, if you approach them for an "Informational Interview" and then try to turn it into a job interview with resume in-hand, they are going to be offended and retract from helping you. Believe me, if you are in a Networking Meeting with someone who needs you, it will occur to this person that you should be talking about his or her organization.

So, the goal of these meetings is to gain advice, guidance, and feedback. Let's learn a little bit more on advice, guidance, and feedback is they relate to the *Human Search Engine*.

Advice: Have you even genuinely been asked for advice from someone? How did you feel? Pretty great, right? They chose you of all people to get advice from which makes you feel as though they respect your opinion. They think of you as an expert on a topic and so you feel even better about the conversation. How long would you be willing to talk to this person if he or she truly wanted nothing from you except your advice?

Guidance: If you want guidance on your job search, who would be a good source? How about professionals who are now working but have been on a job search themselves the last two years? How WILLING do you think someone would be, who has the emotions and experiences of job search fresh in his or her mind, to share some perspective? How did he or she go about a search? Who did she meet with? What did he learn along the way? What would this person do differently?

Feedback: Holding meetings with people close to you who are WILLING to help you produces honest feedback on your presentation style, your message, and your job search strategy. What resonated with them about your presentation? What confused them? Was your message clear? Can they name a couple of organizations that fit the description of the kinds of places you want to work?

> *Believe me, if you are in a Networking Meeting with someone who needs you, it will occur to this person that you should be talking about his or her organization.*

Here's one final lesson before you learn how to conduct Informational Interviews and Networking Meetings. At the end of any meeting, become comfortable asking this question of the person who you are meeting with:

"**Now that you know how I am going about my job search, if you were me (pause)—who would you want to talk to next to continue your search?**" Another way of saying it is: "**If you were me (pause)—what next steps would you take in order to drive your search forward?**" After asking the question, stop talking and let them think. Stay silent. The ideas that these people will come up with for you are astounding! If you've followed the blueprint of connecting accordingly to these individuals, these ideas are going to make you sing and dance! *HSE* works.

TAKE AWAY:

You are now going into important meetings completely armed with a customized, adaptable script that will set the table for your next career. *HSE* gives you a foundation for relevant conversations based on what you need to learn as a result of these meetings. Learning how to masterfully seek advice, guidance, and feedback will serve as the cornerstone of this life-changing foundation.

Chapter 22

MARKETING (YOU)

The *Human Search Engine* INSTRUCTIONAL PROCESS STEP 10:

Showtime! Conducting Informational Interviews & Networking Meetings

Once you have an opportunity to meet with someone through the distinctive process of the *Human Search Engine*, how long will the meeting last? Who will lead the meeting? How will you know if the meeting was effective by way of reaching its goals? How do you ask for advice, guidance, and feedback on your job search?

Answers to these questions will manufacture solutions to landing a rewarding career. They also are automatically part of *HSE*'s process—all of your knowledge on this job search up to this point and a bit more beyond is systematically in place. While even very extroverted people understand the significant nature behind any type of Informational Interview and Networking Meeting, very few understand how to conduct them in a step-by-step process. Remember, these meetings have goals (to be remembered favorably, to receive advice, guidance, and feedback on your search, and to receive referrals by name of people who can advance your search).

I'm about to script the questions to ask, word-for-word, and in the order in which you ask them for these meetings. But first, here are responses to the questions above to give you a solid organizational framework for this step in the *HSE* process—the pinnacle time when job landings can start to take shape (some landings have even occurred during or after this phase, but stick with me—there's a bit more to cover)!

1. How long will these meetings usually last? While you will ask for 20 minutes of his or her time (it's attractive because the number is less than a half hour), these meetings will often last 45 minutes to an hour.

    Check-in with the person who you are meeting with at the 20-minute mark and ask permission to continue. This shows respect for the person's time.

If your meetings are only lasting 20 minutes, my guess is that you're not connecting with people, and you need to revisit how you are presenting yourself. I have had *HSE* clients who asked for 20-minute meetings and end up with one-to-three hour meetings, introductions to other leaders in the organization, plant tours, and even invitations to complete applications that very day.

2. Who will lead these meetings? Just like every other business meeting that you have planned, you are in charge of this meeting. You requested the meeting; you are the one who knows what desired outcomes need come out of it.

   You will drive the meeting, ask the questions, keep it on schedule, and reroute the conversation if it gets off topic. Remember, if you want to present yourself as a professional, then running a focused meeting is a great way to demonstrate your professionalism from the get-go.

   Yes, this is another intentional strategy of *HSE* that puts you under the limelight! It is a subtle, yet demonstrative way, to create a great first impression and showcase the unique you! If you have not run many meetings (or any meetings), the beauty of *HSE* is that it is designed for you to conduct a lot of practice within your network of people before bringing it to center stage.

3. How will you know if the meeting was effective by way of reaching its goals? This is actually very easy to determine. If the person who you meet with provides a referral BY NAME and offers to connect you with this contact, then you know you're on the right track.

   Don't forget another important 'end result' in these meetings as a measuring tool that *HSE's* networking is optimally performing. The person may suggest industries or companies that you should consider in alignment with the types of organizations you want to learn more about.

4. How to ask for advice, guidance, and feedback during these meetings: Here is where we cover the exact questions to ask during your meeting. It is important to use these questions as stated and in the order they are positioned.

   After a few meetings, you may modify these questions a bit based on feedback that you receive. Starting out, however, use this script to take the nervousness out of your initial meetings.

Informational Interview SCRIPT

1. **Thank the interviewee by NAME for meeting with you and give your Focus Statement and your 60-Second Introduction.**

2. **Can you give me an idea of what is going on in the industry right now?** The goal is to get the person talking by asking about something he or she deals with every day. This also helps you uncover problems that need to be solved in this respective industry.

3. **How did you, _____,** (use a personal NAME—be personable when you can) **get involved in this industry?** This question again makes it easy for the person to continue a conversation. The interviewee is discussing a topic that no one knows better than he or she does! Here you may find common ground to navigate the rest of the conversation and perhaps learn pathways into that industry.

4. **What skill sets are important for someone looking to enter this industry?** This is the first moment that you will begin interjecting examples of your skill sets into the conversation. Remember, give enough information to know why you are going to be a great employee.

    For example, of the interviewee says that problem solving is a good trait to have as a project manager, reply as follows, "Well, I'm glad to hear you say that. In my last two positions, analytical problem solving was a big part of my role as a project manager (or whatever title you held—but again, the emphasis here is on skill). Let me give you an example of how we solved a particular problem in my last job (bring this skill to life with a clear, impact-based brief example).

5. **What kind of person succeeds in this industry?** The answer to this question will help you understand the personal traits of a person who fits well in the industry. Now demonstrate those traits with real life examples—again be brief, but succinct. Using summarization skills is the name of the game here. hit on the major points.

6. **What do I need to be aware of during my search—do you have any advice for me as I continue my search?** People love to give advice. they just can't help it. If the interviewee sincerely thinks that you will use his or her advice, the conversation becomes even more productive. The person may talk about his or her last job search. Then, ask if networking is the right way to go about your search. If the response is "yes," then the next question will be hard for the interviewee to ignore.

7. **Clearly, I have a great deal more research to do before making a choice of organizations or an industry. The best way you can help me today is**

by connecting me with other people who would be helpful in my search. If you were me, who do you think it would be important to talk with in order to continue my research? **IMPORTANT:** Know this question word-for-word. Ask it verbatim; it is the most important question of the whole meeting. After asking the question, remain silent.

You will be tempted to talk if there is a moment of silence before the other person answers. Don't talk. Silence is your best friend here. Give the person enough time and respect so he or she can thoroughly deliberate a solid answer. Take just a moment and give yourself 15 seconds of silence right now—I know, it feels a little uncomfortable. If, after this grueling time period that seemed like an eternity, your interviewee cannot offer any names to you, here is a 'back pocket' tool for this situation.

Prior to any Informational Interview, come prepared with a list of 10–15 companies that you can have readily available to share with your interviewee. These companies will represent those within industries you want to work in. The sole purpose of sharing this list is to help jog the memory of your interviewee in terms of identifying people at those organizations.

8. *Ask if it is OK to keep in touch by e-mail,* (NOTE: Every 2–3 weeks you should be sending out a job search update to everyone who you have met with during your search. This update will be a summary of four-five bullet points of the people who you have met with recently, the names of organizations you are interested in learning more about, and a reminder that you are seeking names of people from those companies).

9. *Thank the person for his or her time and promise to keep in touch.* In addition, obtain the interviewee's business card so you have contact information going forward.

That's right, all of this is what you need to accomplish in 20 minutes. To put it in perspective, you need to make a complete stranger who you have been referred to gain your confidence after nearly a half hour. That's not enough. In addition to the interviewee feeling confident about you, he or she must be WILLING to introduce you to other important people. These individuals as part of the special *HSE* networking process could include friends, family members, and colleagues.

Do you now understand why every part of your introduction and achievements are so important to have written, scripted, and practiced? Your ability to connect with these essential people and convince them that you can solve problems, make someone's life easier, and get them closer to reaching goals is the difference between either acquiring a referral by name or becoming just a person's way to pass time.

Please note that without direct name referrals, you have a limited number of people who you can meet with during your search. Through HSE, if you get two direct referrals from each person who you meet with—you literally can never run out of people who are in position to benefit your search. It's a mathematical certainty!

What if I do not get a name referral from my meetings?

This takes us back to the conversation of WILLING and ABLE. There are only two possible reasons that someone does not give you a direct name referral. they were either UNABLE or UNWILLING to do so. While sitting in your car immediately after a meeting where you did not receive any name referrals, it is very important to self-debrief and reconsider if the person was UNABLE or UNWILLING to provide such information.

> *Your ability to connect with these essential people and convince them that you can solve problems, make someone's life easier, and get them closer to reaching goals is the difference between either acquiring a referral by name or becoming just a person's way to pass time.*

If you do not take the time to follow along here step-by-step, you will keep repeating connection mistakes time and time again. You need to adapt to the results of each meeting. Realistically, what are the chances that a business professional who has been in the industry for years doesn't know anyone who you could talk to in his or her field? Frankly, the chances are close to zero. So why didn't this person refer you to someone by name?

They were UNABLE. In this case, based on your delivered message (as sometimes seen in the process), jobseekers make the mistake of not clearly defining themselves and their skill set. Worse, they have regressed and presented themselves as someone who can do "anything for anyone in any circumstance" (that is why it is so important to follow *HSE* as a process from the outset). If your message does not help these key people narrow down the connections in their "mental Rolodex," then you have made it impossible to also narrow their choices based on your definition.

They were UNWILLING. This is a slightly more complex problem. In this case, the person knew exactly what you wanted, but decided not to introduce you to his or her acquaintances. This was because the two of you did not establish a connection, or the other person could not fully understand the value that you could bring to an organization. Regardless of the reason, you need to adjust your presentation if you find yourself on this side of the fence regularly. The other person will basically never say that he or she didn't connect with you or didn't see value in you, simply due to human nature.

This is why it is so important to practice your Informational Interviews with people from your ABC List. These people already know you well and will openly and objectively disclose the truth. As I often say, a real friend is the one who will tell you that you have a piece of celery caught between your teeth.

Who will I be targeting to have these Informational Interviews or Networking Meetings with?

Again, you first need to have four or five of these types of meetings with people from your ABC List before you hold them with someone you don't know well. The saying is, "Start easy, start close to home, but start today." If practice makes perfect, then I want you to make all of your mistakes with people who will render great feedback and are WILLING to help you.

Once you're comfortable from all of the practice, let's examine your target audience for these meetings. These individuals should be one step above the level that you would likely come into an organization. If you're a supervisor, your target will be someone like an operations manager. If you are a salesperson, then you'll want to meet with sales managers.

The rationale here is simple. You want to meet with people who have the problems that you are well equipped to solve. If they understand how you can "solve their problems, make life easier, and get them closer to meeting goals or bonuses," these people will see your value. They also hang out with other sales managers who have similar problems that you could solve. Lastly, sales managers, for example, are most often responsible for hiring sales people.

Through HSE, if you get two direct referrals from each person who you meet with—you literally can never run out of people who are in position to benefit your search. It's a mathematical certainty!

If people network with others at their same level (project managers meets with project managers), you run the risk of being a threat to the person you're meeting with. *It is very important to meet with people who are responsible for solving the problems that you are uniquely qualified to solve.*

How does HSE change if I'm having a Networking Meeting instead of an Informational Interview?

As discussed earlier, Networking Meetings are different than Informational Interviews. Networking Meetings are less about specific industry information and more about meeting with people who know others for a living. Examples of this demographic would be salespeople, pastors, public relations professionals, elected officials, educators, and small business owners. Basically, I am referring to folks who work in a "people profession."

Think about the last group of career people mentioned above. why small business owners? These people do not have big advertising budgets; if they don't network, their business dies. They will understand exactly how you are going about your search. You probably won't even have to explain it to them. They go about finding customers the same way you are doing your job search.

Instead of asking questions about specific industries or companies (as we did with the Informational Interview questions), focus on explaining the type of person you want to meet with and why you can help a business. What is this person's personality like? What position(s) do they hold in the community? Help the person narrow down their massive "mental Rolodex." These people know many individuals, but if you don't narrow this thought process down for them, they will rightfully struggle to pinpoint the one or two individuals who are ideal for you to meet with.

With Networking Meetings you will likely have no idea where the conversation will go. After giving your Focus Statement and 60-Second Introduction, let the conversation flow. Talk about who does that type of work and why. Focus on people types, not job types. "People who know people" for a living often characterize people by type, not by profession.

Also, be sure to concentrate on people who have careers that depend on their ability to network. Since this is a different way of doing a job search, "networking with people who network for a living" will make this a great deal easier for you. You will likely not need to go into a long spiel of how you are doing your search because networking and connecting is nothing new to these people. You will have the opportunity to start your discussion by sharing insight with the other person on how networking contributed toward his or her job search success.

The significance here is that the rest of the job search world (until they read this book) is trying to land a career by way of posted job ads and Internet searches. Even traditional jobseekers who try networking "for sake of networking" or novelty, find that the ones they converse with cannot assist them with their search unless they know of an open job or someone who has hiring authority. Remember, networking is not about collecting the most business cards or meeting a lot of strangers and then hoping for a miracle. Trying to explain the *HSE* process of job search to someone who has never done it this way is like talking to a cow about flying. People who have never experienced this method have no point of reference to discuss it.

The above example of unskilled networking is due to both the jobseeker and interviewee's misunderstanding of its true purpose. Contrast this longtime, common expectation of networking with anyone who networks for a living. They immediately understand the importance of networking and the value it can deliver in business. They quickly understand the kinds of people who use it to make their best sales or connections, and it is done strikingly similar to the *HSE* way. The most common response when you network with someone who does it for a living is, "I understand what you are doing, and I think you are going about it in the right way. Please describe the kind of people who would be helpful for you to be in front of."

The last idea I want to leave you with on the topic of networking is to include people who have been unemployed in the past few years and successfully found a new position. There is value in connecting with these individuals as well (I see it every day though *HSE* because we have built such a strong network from ground up the past three years. Our "landers" keep in touch and help others!). What did they do to find their new position? Who did they meet with? How did they determine which companies or industries they should focus on? Did they utilize a strategically-planned form of job search or was their landing random? In a way, this networking meeting is also an Informational Interview, isn't it?

If the goal is to talk to people who "live in the world that you want to live in next," then what could you learn from someone who has just gone through what you are experiencing? Perhaps the most common mistake people make in job search is they attempt to do it on their own. Without these types of discussions, aren't you destined to make the same mistakes that others have made? Why not learn from their experiences?

Keep this saying in mind: "Unless you are inventing something, don't ever do anything for the first time. Find someone who has already done it and learn from his or her experiences." Let that one sink in for a moment. Don't let your ego get in the way here. Remember, people want to help you on your job search, but they don't know how. You need to continuously teach them how to help.

Networking Meeting SCRIPT:

1. *Thank the person by NAME for meeting with you and give your 60-Second Introduction.*
2. *Clearly state that the goal of today's meeting and the best way for him or her to help you is by receiving a referral (or referrals), BY NAME, of people who they think could talk to you about your search.*
3. *Ask the person to tell you a little about themselves.* Remind the person who referred you and why. Ask questions about how networking helped foster success in his or her career.
4. *Describe the type of organization that you are ultimately hoping to land with* (size, industry, publicly held, family owned, etc., and any industries of interest).

   Now, ask the person, "With the organizational description I just provided, could you please list two or three organizations in our area that fit this industry?" This helps ensure that the idea of what you are looking for mirrors the image of what he or she is thinking about—in other words, it's so both of you are on the same page.
5. *Describe the type of position you are hoping to land in terms of duties, responsibilities, authority, and level.* Now, ask for an example of a job that comes to mind (it does NOT need to be an open job) that fits the description of what you hope to be doing in your next position.
6. *Give examples of achievements to validate that your skill set is appropriate for the position you are seeking.* Watch for signs (verbal and nonverbal) from the other person that signify you will be a good fit for an organization.
7. Once any validation of your value or fit (for an organization) is demonstrated (again, verbally or nonverbally), ask specifically for BY NAME for referrals. *"I want to again thank you very much for meeting with me today. As I mentioned, I am networking with leaders in this area to do my job search. The best way for you to help me today is to provide a referral or two of someone who could help advance my job search. If you were me (pause), who do you think it would be important for me to meet with in the next few days for advice and guidance on my search?"*
8. Once you receive a referral (DON'T do this until you have received a referral), *ask if he or she would be WILLING to include you in any other emails in which you were being referred to someone else moving forward.* Then you can directly follow up with that referral. Again, this is a passive (yet

important) alternative, so we don't want to focus on this step before exhausting the proactive way of receiving referrals (as opposed to you being referred on to someone else). Get the names when you can!

9. *Ask if there is any additional advice about your job search before the two of you part.*
10. *Thank the person again for his or her time and promise to keep in touch.*

Again, relevant networking is neither an art form nor an exact science. While you will likely develop your own string of questions after doing a number of networking meetings, and that is a good sign of progress, I advise you to start by using the above script as written. People new to networking usually are quite nervous, and therefore don't really drive the conversation in any measurable direction that helps them. Without a script, people will have a number of very nice conversations, but they will not receive any specific advice or BY NAME referrals. Without this type of information from the people who you are networking with, how do you keep your search going in the right direction?

TAKE AWAY:

For your Informational Interviews and Networking Meetings, you now have a timely, well-organized, and almost failsafe script to get out and shake some trees that are ripe with connections! Remember our math problem. If you get two BY NAME referrals from each person who you meet with through these meetings, it is mathematically impossible for you to run out of people to network with on your search. See how so many people are landing meaningful careers the *HSE* way!

Chapter 23
MARKETING (YOU)

The *Human Search Engine*
INSTRUCTIONAL PROCESS STEP 11:

The Networking Brief:
Whatever you give people is how they'll know you.

Now your calendar is busy with practicing those *Human Search Engine* scripts for Informational Interviews and Networking Meetings. It feels good again to have your calendar full, doesn't it? Well, it's about to get even busier. I know you'd rather be working in a new career in which you have a say in actually creating; like most *HSE* success stories. you're getting closer to that realization. For now, I'm sure the taste of success is feeling a lot more realistic than it did before you started reading this book. Keep practicing.

So, while you're in fine-tuning mode for these meetings, how do you actually put those scripts into action? Remember, in order to get hired you need to be talking to people in your industry. That means the only reason to network through *HSE*'s Informational Interviews and Networking Meetings is to gain referrals (or be referred as a secondary, passive resort) from people in your industry for the sole end result of landing a rewarding career.

Consider for a moment this process from the perspective of the people who you are about to meet with in Networking Meetings or Informational Interviews. Whether you are about to meet with someone who you have known your entire life or with a complete stranger as a result of a referral, the success of the meeting will be determined by your ability to "paint a picture."

The individual who you are meeting with must gain a good sense of what kind of person you are, along with an understanding of the skills and achievements you can offer your next employer. He or she also needs to understand what type of organization you hope to "land" with next. If the person is confused with any part of your presentation, he or she will be UNABLE to narrow down the "mental Rolodex" in order to give you BY NAME referrals.

Surprisingly, this is a pretty easy concept to grasp if you are meeting with a complete stranger. What most people miss in the *HSE* process is that this notion is doubly tough if you are meeting with someone who you have known a long time. While this sounds counterintuitive, really think about how those types of people know you. Do they really know you based on your career path, your duties, and work-related achievements, or do they know you because you have been social buddies on weekends for the past five years? They may know whether you like olives in your martini or tartar sauce with your fish on Friday night (Friday fish fries are a big Wisconsin thing by the way). You have spent hundreds of hours with them, but what do they know about you as an employee?

We need to make sure that people who are WILLING to help us are also ABLE to help us. Unless we help them understand who we are as a potential employee—a professional, olives and tartar sauce in 10-gallon pales aren't going to help them at all when it comes to trying to assist you. This concept became very real to me when it happened with one of my best friends.

Phil is a terrific and compassionate school administrator in my geographical area. He is as good a person as he is a friend. Among all the people I come across in my profession, Phil is genuinely one of the best people I have ever met. Every year during the past decade, both of our families share a weeklong summer getaway in a small cottage in northern Wisconsin. With eight people crammed into a two-bedroom cottage for a week, let's just say being friends is one thing, but seeing one another at 6 a.m. with tussled hair and in pajamas means you know them at a very different level.

During our annual "cottage" week, Phil and I also spend time together fishing. We discuss EVERYTHING. Children, marriage, finances, parents, and growing older are among the endless topics we discuss. There is no limit to our deep friendship and the value we place on each other's advice. Let's just say we KNOW each other.

In 2008, I walked away from the paper industry to start teaching career search on a full-time basis. I had been doing it in one form or another since 2002, so Phil and I had talked about this over the years at the cottage. As you can imagine, Phil's connections within local school systems could be very valuable to me as I started to contact high schools about speaking to students.

I thought that one conversation with Phil, my best and WILLING friend, would lead me to connecting with principals across the area, and with his referrals I would be "in like Flynn." When I casually asked Phil if he would connect me with regional administrators so I could tell them about my work, his response shocked me. "Why do you want to meet with them?" he asked. "What is it exactly that you do, and why do you need to talk to them?"

I was momentarily floored. My good friend was not opening up his mental Rolodex to me. Why? Wasn't I good enough? Wasn't I smart enough? Did he think I would embarrass him in front of his colleagues? Maybe he thought I lacked experience. All sorts of awful ideas traveled through my head. For just a moment I thought, "If he really was my friend, he would be falling all over himself to help me!"

Instead of becoming mad or shutting down, I decided to help Phil understand me in a different light. Subsequently, Phil and I talked in-depth about my work. The discussion included what I could bring as value to students. Suddenly, he opened up to helping me. As his knowledge of my professional situation grew, so did his WILLINGNESS to help me get in front of the right people.

We had a great conversation in which he not only gave me BY NAME referrals, but he helped me better understand how public schools operated and the best ways to contact people there. Wow, out of all those conversations in the boat while we were fishing that included work as a general topic, there was still enough lack of understanding between us to cause a real eye-opening moment for me. and hopefully for you.

> *We need to make sure that people who are WILLING to help us are also ABLE to help us.*

From this story, remember two lessons:

- People only know you the way they know you (don't assume anything)
- People want to help you with your job search, but they don't know how; we need to teach them how they can best help us.

Enter the Networking Brief

A Networking Brief is a document that you will email to the person who you are going to have an Informational Interview or Networking Meeting with about 48 hours BEFORE the meeting. The goal of the Networking Brief is to frame the flavor of the conversation ahead of time so there is a certain expectation between the two of you before meeting in person.

The two of you can hit the ground running with a clear understanding of who you are, what you are looking for, your achievements, and organizations of interest. Networking Briefs should be one page, and again, email is the preferred method of submittal in case the person who you are meeting with wants to forward it on for additional contact and networking purposes on your behalf.

The Networking Brief contains four main parts:

1. A summary of your job search objective (this comes from your 60-Second Introduction)
2. A list of achievements (which you have already documented as part of the *HSE* process in Chapter 11) that demonstrate you have the skills for success in your next career
3. A list of your technical and people (soft) skills that will allow you to be successful in the job you are seeking (refer to Chapter 12 for additional information)
4. Organizations of interest. This list of 10-15 organizations in the surrounding area that you would like to learn more about will help spur the person's memory of people they know. The list also serves as a complementary confirmation regarding the types of organizations that you have been trying to describe to the interviewee.

The Networking Brief will be an evolving document as you learn more during your *HSE* job search research project. You will add and subtract organizations, change skills and achievements that you choose to present per each respective unique opportunity, and so on. Your search objective will change a little too based on what you experience as well. Remember, this document isn't for you. it is for the people who you are about to meet with.

Amazing things happen when you give people the opportunity to mentally prepare for these conversations. I do hear on occasion *HSE* jobseekers who attend a meeting after they sent a Networking Brief and find that the other person already had names readily to share with them!

Addendum: Refer to page 165 *for a sample Networking Brief*

TAKE AWAY:

Regardless of your relationship—from complete stranger to someone you think knows you very well, and everyone in between, framing any conversation off of a Networking Brief makes the discussion more effective, efficient, and purposeful for both parties.

Chapter 24

UNIT RECAP: Marketing

1. Create your job search marketing pieces: Tagline, Focus Statement, 60-Second Introduction, and Networking Brief.

2. Using the list of networking questions from the book, conduct your first Networking Meetings with people on your 1000/1000 List. These will be your first major interactions, so you will be a bit nervous and unsure of the process—that's why we are doing them with people who are incredibly WILLING to help you. Explain to these people that the meetings are practice runs for you, but that they can significantly help you with your job search by actively participating and referring you to other people to network with.

3. After your first meeting, ask the person what overall message was received during the dialogue. Was it clear to this person why you asked to talk? Does this person understand how to help you with your search (through information and referrals)? After you described the type of organization that you were looking to come into contact with, could he or she make a short list of organizations that fit said description (this ensures that the message this person receives is the same message you intended to send). At the end of each of your networking meetings, ask your 1000/1000 List person to create an ABC list of his or her own detailing the names, position held, and how he or she knows them. Ask to send that list to you in a day or so, so you can identify which of the people on his or her list you would like this person to connect you to.

4. Now conduct three-to-four job search Networking Meetings with people "who think you are awesome." Focus on meeting with people like former co-workers, bosses, neighbors, mentors, etc.—those who already think very positively about you.

5. Start conducting Networking Meetings with individuals on your B and C List. focus on people who are WILLING to help you first (even though you can't immediately identify whether they are ABLE to help you.)

These will be either Informational Interviews (if you are talking to people in the target organizations or industry) or Networking Meetings with a focus on asking people you know to get you to people in your target industry. The focus is always ongoing research. Never ask anyone if they can "get you in" somewhere. that will turn them off very quickly.

6. Once you have done five or six Networking Meetings and are starting to feel comfortable with the process, set up meetings with people on your A List. Explain to them how you are going about your job search. These people will identify with it right away because they would likely do a search the same way, given their position in the workplace. Ask specifically for referrals to other A List people, including hiring managers and business owners. Ask them to evaluate your presentation and solicit constructive guidance on how your message came across. Ask them for feedback on your Networking Brief and to focus their referrals on your Target List of organizations.

7. The goal is to receive not less than two "by name" referrals from each person you hold a networking meeting with. You are talking with people who want to assist you; let them know the best way to help you is through these introductions. At the end of the meeting when you ask for referrals, be sure to have your Networking Brief on the table in front of you to help this person identify organizations of interest.

8. As you begin meeting with people who you have been referred to by your 1000/1000 and ABC Lists, be sure to approach them only after your contact has e-mailed or called to make the connection for you. Once that is done, send the person who you were referred to a networking meeting request via email, and attach your Networking Brief to the email (which makes it easy for these people to forward if they decide to). If the person doesn't respond to your request to meet, ask your connection (who referred you to them) to contact them and encourage a meeting with you. Again, the goal is two referrals from each person you meet with. Getting at least two makes it impossible for you to run out of people to meet with before you land your next position.

9. Continue applying for posted jobs, but only apply for positions that truly fit. Spend only about 25% of your time responding to posted positions. For measuring your activity, use 20 hours per week as your target goal, not including any time applying for or researching posted jobs. Twenty hours a week setting up and conducting Networking Meetings and Informational Interviews is what to aim for. Your target should be holding five meetings per week. Meet with three people each week who

you already know and two people each week who you don't know, but have been directly referred to.

10. Evaluate weekly whether your activity is leading you closer to your goal. Are the conversations getting you closer to your target organizations or people? If not, it's time to refocus and recalibrate. Don't confuse activity with progress. does it feel like your work is getting you closer to the people who have the problems you can solve for them? If you are not getting closer, do you need to redefine your message?

11. Identify and join a local job search support group. Share with others in the group how you are going about your search. Teach this process to another jobseeker as an introduction to something different. As you teach it to them, you will understand the process at a very different level. Refer them to *HSE* though this read.

12. Create a complete and professional LinkedIn profile. Begin connecting with people on your ABC List through LinkedIn. Review their connections for people you would like to connect with for networking or Informational Interviews.

13. Track your activity and progress on a chart that you review with our accountability person or group. Evaluate and adjust your activity based on progress towards the goal.

14. Limit non-value added activities like TV (two hours/day max.) Volunteer during each week to stay active and facilitate connections. Stay physically active.

15. Become active in community groups to facilitate connections. Avoid isolation at all costs.

16. If your search stalls, reconnect with former co-workers and 100/100 List people. Restart the process from scratch, if needed.

Chapter 25

HITTING THE STREETS

Post Instruction : Accountability Groups Provide You with Street Smarts to Land Your Next Job

I am a huge fan of Accountability Groups during the *Human Search Engine* journey, which is now post-instructional in nature and more concentrated on pounding the pavement to find your next career. Remember, though, that all of the preceding steps are subject to modification, adaptation, and learned perseverance. So, theoretically, we're always learning and applying knowledge!

Everything I have experienced through *HSE* suggests that the number one factor in moving the job search forward after the step-by-step instruction is joining or forming an Accountability Group. This is a set of three-to-five *HSE* jobseekers who meet weekly to review their job search efforts, develop new ideas and leads for each other, and hold one other accountable for doing what needs to be done at 8:00 a.m. every morning for the next seven days. The people in your group should come from different backgrounds and industries so there are new views of the world for you to explore. You should also only invite people into your Accountability Group who represent opinions that you respect.

The two greatest motivators in job search are shame and fear. Don't get me wrong. in everyday life these are not desirable motivators. The *HSE* process intentionally asks people to step out of their comfort zone. Consequently, this process has a built-in mechanism to influence jobseekers to act upon something they are not used to doing—all for the better.

There is no shame in being unemployed if you are working hard to solve that issue. Shame, however, is a great motivator if you have to report in front of people who you respect that you didn't do what you promised to. The fear of looking people who you trust and respect in the eye and telling them that you didn't work hard on your job search is usually enough to get people to act.

In these meetings you will not only share ideas and help each other on your searches, but you will also promise the group a certain level of activity that you need to report on the following week. In most cases, the fear and shame of disappointing the group is enough for you to overcome your hesitation in making connections and having the conversations with people you promised. Think of it as a pledge. I can tell you from experience that is why *HSE* is one of the strongest, most resolute human networks around. inarguably (more on that in the end of this book).

People in Accountability Groups need to be firm, but fair. The group's goal is never to punish inactivity with harsh words or guilt, but to investigate the core reasons for stagnation and then provide support and solutions. The goal for everyone in the group is the same. to find their next great career opportunity. On any given day, your contribution to the group might result in a connection to help someone else, or it could take the shape of a compassionate listening ear to cushion the blow of a job interview that didn't end favorably. Moreover, on any given day, from these meetings you could LAND a great career!

Accountability Individuals

It is possible to have a single person be your Accountability Group, although I highly recommend going with two groups—one would be an individual who you respect and the other is a group of three-to-five current jobseekers serving as an Accountability Group. The individual serves as more of a mentor or a coach, and the Accountability Group offers diverse perspectives, but both dynamics are similar in their essential functions. Who you select as your accountability person is very important. There are three traits this person must have:

- Employment and be free of any personal or professional crisis.
- An ability to assertively and objectively speak the truth to you. Sometimes the disclosures may be difficult to share, yet you know he or she will converse in a respectful and supportive way.
- Personal and professional opinions of you that must matter to you.

> **Without this type of relationship the person will be just another face for you to complain to about what you're going through. The individual's ability to motivate you comes without words because your respect for this person is that strong.**

In order for anyone to serve as your accountability individual you also must have a very high opinion of this person. Just the idea of disappointing this person should make your skin crawl. You should be sweating bullets if you had to tell this person you didn't conduct the *HSE* business you promised to do. These are important points. Without this type of relationship the person will be just another face for you to complain to about what you're going through. The individual's ability to motivate you comes without words because your respect for this person is that strong.

Who might qualify as your accountability individual?

- A former boss or coach who was your mentor in the past
- A 1000/1000 List person who has shown the ability to lovingly kick your butt for good reason
- A religious leader for whom you have tremendous respect
- Your father-in-law or mother-in-law (your own father and mother might be too close to you to create the positive pressure you need)
- A brother or sister who leads other people or business processes for a living

It generally does not work very well to have your spouse or significant other be your accountability person. These people care for you at the deepest level and may have the tendency to say, "Oh it's all right. you'll do better next time." There are moments in the *HSE* process where you need such doses of unconditional support and caring; the accountability part isn't one of those times.

TAKE AWAY:

Start forming and/or joining an Accountability Group. As people, we are hard wired to not disappoint others who are meaningful to us. Again, especially this late in the *HSE* process, don't forge ahead alone.

Chapter 26

HITTING THE STREETS

Post Instruction: Streets with Detours. Your GPS is *HSE*. The common mistakes in this job search that you will make.

This chapter is your blueprint for navigating through some detours which are expected to happen. Some readers of *Human Search Engine* may already have landed a new, rewarding career if they've followed the steps and done the work as outlined. If that's the case, I congratulate them! The process works, and it lands success for people at different times based on any number of circumstances, including timing. For the rest of you, keep doing the work.

The following is a list of detours that you've already encountered or may confront, along with guidelines to resolve these bumps in the road:

Activity vs. Progress (needed activity levels defined)

- The level of activity that you need to successfully use the *HSE* process is easy to define. You will work on it 20 hours per week, but only two of those hours can be spent searching and applying for jobs online.
- The other 18 hours per week must consist of face-to-face Informational Interviews or Networking Meetings, company research from business databases like Reference USA or Hoovers (available at your local library), or setting up said meetings above.
- You must meet each week with three people who know you (networking for job search introductions to people they know) and two meetings with people who can help you with your search (with information or referrals) that you didn't know when the week started.
- The key to meeting with people though is to track progress, not just chart activity. If you are not meeting with people inside your industries of interest, and instead meeting with a lot of random people, the referrals you receive will likely not bring you closer to talking with individuals who need you to solve their problems. Remember, each referral should

bring you closer to talking with "people who live in the world that you want to live in" for your next job.

- While you may start with people not in your industry or job type (your 1000/1000 List and ABC List), the goal is to receive referrals from these persons. You can use these referrals to talk to others who do the same type of work you do or work in an industry that you want to be in. If you're not attaining this goal, it's time to revisit your job search Focus Statement and make it clear to people who you would like to be introduced to.

Determining which ABC List people can help you before meeting with them

- The most challenging jobseekers I work with are engineers, accountants, and some information technology professionals. These are very smart people, but their training has taught them to always think linearly to get from point A to point B. People like this tend to look at most things either 'black or white.' This type of thinking leads them to evaluate the value of the people who they will be meeting with before the conversation even takes place. Whether this happens prior to the meeting or at the outset of the dialogue, this is a HUGE mistake. The *HSE* process is a research project and a constant quest for discovering information; therefore, IT IS WHAT YOU *THINK* YOU KNOW that will keep you from having the most valuable job search meetings.

- Not meeting with your brother-in-law because you don't know exactly what he does for a living keeps you from the 500 people in his mental Rolodex. Not meeting with the leader of your religious organization because it is "too touchy/feely for business" keeps you from the 1000 people in his mental Rolodex. Not having this conversation with your spouse because you believe "if he or she could have helped me on my search, he or she would have done so already" makes the most significant and WILLING person in your life unable to help you.

- Some of the most amazing *HSE* job-landing stories that I have witnessed started with the disclosure, "I wasn't even sure why we were meeting and what we were going to discuss in terms of helping my job search, but I knew the other person was WILLING to help if he or she could." People want to help you with your job search, but they don't know how. Continue to teach them that the best way they can help you is with a referral to others.

Trying to be Gumby

- During your job search, you will naturally encounter some indecisive moments. Out of human nature, you will be tempted to mold yourself into being a viable candidate for positions that you already know don't match either your interests or qualifications. In *HSE* terms, I call this "trying to be Gumby." Out of frustration or not knowing what else to do, you try to convince hiring managers of organizations that you are something that you are not in order to end the pain of unemployment.

- As the old saying goes, "when you are a hammer, everything looks like a nail." When you are unemployed and scared, every job looks like a good job. this is how people end up in careers that are a bad fit.
- If you need to take a short-term job that isn't a great fit in order to keep food on the table and the lights on in your house, that is understandable. But realize that this job is not your final destination; it is simply buying you time to enact the entire *HSE* program. You take this job to finance the rest of your search and your life.

Using *HSE* the wrong way (to obtain direct job interviews)

- All too often jobseekers use this process as some trick to get in front of hiring managers so they present themselves as a potential employee. *HSE* is tactfully and intelligently designed to not place its jobseekers in front of hiring managers as a full-court press for them to make a direct hiring decision. WARNING: People who try to use the *HSE* process as a "left-hand sell" job to potential employers will remain unemployed a really long time, because their search is based on deception or lying.
- Hiring managers understand the process that I am trying to teach you better than you do. They likely used (or are familiar with) many parts of this process themselves and know how it is supposed to work. Trying to fool people into interviewing you by sneaking in the door under the disguise of a networking meeting tells them one thing about you. It reveals that you are willing to sacrifice your personal and professional integrity. How many of those types of people are hired under this approach?
- Use the process correctly in front of hiring managers and you will typically hear, "You are going about this the right way." Use the process incorrectly by tricking your way inside an organization and you will more than likely hear the door closing hard behind you while leaving the meeting.

Not keeping the pipeline full

- Think of this job search as creating a wave of constant activity. If the biggest problems you have with your job search are that nobody knows you exist and you are unaware of at least 85% of organizations in your area, then solving those two problems are creating that wave.

- That wave requires constant activity that lets people who are unaware of you know that you exist, are available, and are talented.
- That wave of constant activity has people talking about you and your search in lunch conversations and next to water coolers.
- That wave has hiring managers talking about you when they ask each other, "Who's available right now?" If you create enough conversations about your search, news of your availability will eventually reach the ears of the person that needs you to solve his or her problems on behalf of a company.
- Creating that wave requires dozens of conversations. To go from unknown to known in the minds of hiring managers takes a lot of activity. The average HSE jobseeker will have about 25 Informational Interviews or Networking Meetings before they land (some have landed with fewer, while others have taken longer, but this is a measurement to aim for).
- The hardest conversation I have with people is after a "sure thing" job opportunity falls through. They were so sure about a job offer that they stopped their networking activity. They let the wave crash.
- I see their sad eyes and they say, "I don't know what to do next." I reply, "You know exactly what you need to do next. You just won't like the answer very much. Go refill the pipeline of people to talk to and recreate the wave of activity that you had two weeks ago."
- And so they need to start from scratch, and that is more than all right to do, if needed. It just takes much longer and more effort to get restarted. Remember, until you have a job offer in hand, you have nothing. keep the process going.

Poor or no tracking along the way and trying to fly solo
- When is the last time that you completed a project without planning the needed steps and tracking your progress against them as a guide? If the boss from your last job gave you a project and you didn't give him or her an update on it against a timeline, how did that conversation go?
- Timelines exist in project management to hold people accountable to achieve specific goals by certain times. Some tasks need to be completed before other essential ones can even begin. Without tracking your progress toward established goals and a timeline, you are just taking random actions and hoping for a good result.
- Again, commit to 20 hours a week with only two of those hours on the computer or applying for posted job ads. Meet with no less than

five people per week, face-to-face. Three of these individuals you should already know and two will consist of referrals from others.
- Create profiles of organizations that fit your career passion and research these companies in order to be able to approach them for referrals. Follow the networking meeting concepts and steps outlined in Chapters 21 & 22, and seek help from others while showing your value in solving workplace problems.
- I challenge you to do each of these tactical steps as prescribed and not fly solo looking for random opportunities. Make your opportunities count instead of relying on a hole-in-one. Share your progress and timelines with others (Chapter 25) to let them hold you accountable in a friendly and supportive way.

Expecting others to advance your search for you

- Who is the person that is most motivated to solve your job search problem? I trust you answered, YOU! Even though *HSE* jobseekers rely on people who are WILLING to help as part of the process, it is important to note that the only person who is totally committed to helping you find your next opportunity. is you.
- An observation that would be helpful here is for me to ask you to think about your best friend in the entire world. This person is probably on your 1000/1000 List. You would do almost anything for one other. You have known each other a long time. this is your go-to person when you have a difficult problem to solve or even address a sensitive family issue.
- Now ask yourself these questions: How much time do you spend thinking about your best friend when you are not around this person? Do you wake up in the middle of the night worried about how this person's job is going? Do you have moments during the day when you worry about how your best friend will pay for his or her college tuition? The answer is probably. no.
- For better or worse, right or wrong, we are all too tied up in our own lives and with our family to spend any real time worrying about someone else. especially when we are not with them regularly. With this in mind, I want you to think about what happens if you ask the people who are WILLING to help you for assistance in your job search and then don't follow up to keep them engaged.
- We have a tendency to believe that after we talk to people who are WILLING to help us with our job search, they are "on assignment" for us 24/7.

- After all, aren't they actively making contacts for you when you are not around them? Aren't they dutifully scoping out job possibilities and making notes of companies they think you should contact along the way? Again, when even your best friend is not around, how much time do you spend worry about what is going on in his or her life?
- This is why it is important for you to consistently check in with these people (your 1000/1000 List, ABC List, and those who make up your Accountability Groups) as outlined in *HSE* to update them on your search.
- "Out of sight, out of mind" is a phrase you should remember in this context. The only way these key contacts will be constantly on the lookout for possibilities (people or companies) is if you keep them updated on your progress. Meet with these people (your closest ABC List people, for starters) every two weeks over lunch (you buy). You can even send these people email updates (as referenced with Accountability Groups in Chapter 25). Think of it as playing "reporter" by providing news updates on your job search!
- Remember, if these individuals don't hear from you in several weeks, they may very well assume a talented person like you has already landed a position and not think about your search at all anymore. It is your job to keep the people who are WILLING to help you actively engaged for the duration of your search.

If your search stalls, are you UNWILLING or UNABLE to continue?

- Almost predictably, your job search efforts will stall somewhere along the way. If you recall, you go through the process steps that help you into the Definition stage. Then you dig right into the RESEARCH stage as you become aware of organizations that you never knew existed. Even in the MARKETING stage, you will meet with people close to you with great fervor and anticipation. You will receive referrals and be referred to others, and your *HSE* job search will be on a roll. and then the wheels fall off.
- Whether it is having trouble getting a response from someone who you are trying to meet with or hitting a brick wall getting in front of someone at the company of your dreams, you will find yourself at a point where you look in the mirror and say, "What do I do next?" Analyzing this question and breaking the answer into "UNWILLING or UNABLE" is the best way to get you restarted.

- When you are stuck during your search, find out if you really don't know what to do, or if you are just UNWILLING at the moment to do what needs to be done. Frustration with the job search process is different than not knowing what to do next.
- If you truly have "hit the wall" in your job search, hold a couple of "sure thing" meetings. These are meetings with people who you have already met with during your search and are incredibly WILLING to help you. Update them on the last five meetings (Networking or Informational Interviews). Let them review your recent research and ask these folks for ideas. Describe to them what you have learned during this process along with what has surprised you.
- You might want to have one of these meetings with your spouse or significant other. It always amazes me how underutilized these people are during job search. Who could be more motivated to help you during this time?
- You may also be shocked that some of your spouse's connections can lead you to people to meet with as well. Everyone has a "mental Rolodex" of people who you don't know. Make sure to take the time to teach your significant other that connecting you with people is the best way he or she can help you.
- If the answer to your question is that you are truly "UNABLE" to continue the process (genuinely don't know what to do next), then start again with the MARKETING phase (beginning in Chapter 18). You may even need a refresher from the RESEARCH unit (Chapters 15-17).
- After what you have learned from the Networking Meetings and Informational Interviews, what do you now see differently from your research? Present your research to someone else and ask this person to reach some conclusions for you based on what you have learned. Meet with your Accountability individual or group and review your conclusions with them as well.
- In the MARKETING phase of *HSE* the task is to meet with people to discuss your search. It is not possible to "run out of people to talk to." In the Fox River Valley, for example, there are more than 250,000 people who live here. When a jobseeker comes to me and says, "I've talked with everyone that I can," how do you think I respond? With just a whiff of productive sarcasm, I just reply, "Tell me about the first 500 people who you met with."

- Usually when people think they are "UNABLE" to do anything more with their search, they really need to just expand their view of who is available to potentially talk to and what is around in terms of organizations.
- Can you imagine a salesperson coming back to his or her sales manager and saying, "There's no one left to sell to; I've talked to everyone." New ideas will not always come from your own perspective. You hit a brick wall because you exhausted basically all of the possibilities in your perspective. Help others find new perspectives and new possibilities for you.

Disregarding PIPs (Previously Important People)

Karl is a retired teacher and another one of my very close friends. We became close friends while both rehabilitating from back surgeries. We spent almost three months walking nearly five miles regularly as part of our recovery. As you might imagine with that much time together, we got to know each other very well. Karl is one of my 1000/1000 List people. I hope each of you have a "Karl" in your life. my life is much better because I do.

One day as we were talking, Karl used the word 'PIP' (remember, from Chapter 18) while he was discussing a group of people that he was hanging out with. I had never heard the word so I asked him what it meant. He replied, "Previously Important People." I laughed a little at the phrase and asked him to describe what he meant by it.

Karl described this group of people as retired individuals who used to be very connected and held influential jobs in the area. Twenty years ago these were the movers and shakers in their areas of expertise. These men and women spent the better part of their lives in board rooms and council meetings where big ideas were made and implemented.

Now in their retirement years, these people value simpler things like freedom, experiences, and sharing all of their hard-earned knowledge. Unfortunately, with all of that knowledge to give, very few are willing to ask for their advice, guidance, and feedback. As *HSE* jobseekers though, we know better. We know that these individual's experiences and connections are critical to our success.

- Learn about the nationwide organization, SCORE (Service Corps. Of Retired Executives). The organization has local chapters, and the group's sole purpose is to make available the wisdom and experience of retired executives to the next generation. It is an incredible idea. If we don't ask for advice from people who were faced with similar problems at one time, we are destined to make all of the mistakes they did. Why not learn from their experiences?

- Not only do these people have great life experiences to draw from, but they also remain deeply connected in the community through volunteer and philanthropic work. The people that they knew—AND STILL KNOW—may be the exact type of person who you need to talk to.
- Retired people have done job searches themselves and can give great guidance on how they did theirs successfully. How did they go about it? Who did they meet with? What would these people do today if they had to do a search on their own? It is true for all people—ask for their advice and they will talk all day. In the case of PIPS, retired individuals actually have time for you when they're not out making the world a better place by helping others.
- Relationships don't end when someone retires. it just takes on a different form. In this more advanced form of relational networking, retired people can easily meet with their connections and ask if they would be WILLING to meet with you.
- What you are about to find out is that these people aren't PREVIOUSLY important people at all. They are vibrant, CURRENTLY important people who have the flexibility in their schedules to get involved in your search (if you can prove to them why you are worth helping. hint, hint, go about as *HSE* has scripted).

Trading perfect inaction for imperfect action

The last mistake you are about to make in your search is not doing anything until your presentation or choice of person to meet with is EXACTLY right. I call that perfect inaction.

In doing the primary *HSE* steps (Definition, Research, and Marketing), you will have ample opportunity to constantly improve your Focus Statement or do additional research. People can fall into the trap of spending dozens of hours perfecting their 60-Second Introduction without ever getting in front of anyone to actually deliver it to. They can spend 100 hours or more on researching organizations that might have the problems that they can solve, yet never actually approach any of them.

If anything, understand this: In order to land your next job you need to be talking to someone face-to-face at some point. Even when jobseekers send resumes, their ultimate goal is to ask for a job interview. *HSE* is all about creating those face-to-face conversations from a different angle, but the goal is the same—talking to people. The more time you spend perfecting your message, the less time you are actually delivering that message to someone who can help you.

Let's be clear, I want you to spend enough time doing each one of the *HSE* steps that prepares you to meet with people; don't short change that. On the other hand, you can also see that sitting in your basement changing three words in an objective instead of meeting with someone could be easier. I have a word for that. HIDING.

The greatest psychological human fear is not being important to anyone or anything. The second greatest fear is that of being judged by others. I fully understand why people primp and preen their presentations to the point that they never hold a meeting. They are scared. That is the entire reason for starting with people who are incredibly WILLING to help you.

I promise you will make mistakes with your first Networking Meetings. That's why you hold the first ones with people who like and believe in you already. If you make a mistake—so what? It doesn't have to be perfect for them to help you. Make your mistakes during these practice runs so that by the time you are meeting with people who you don't know, your presentation is polished and confident. You will be better the third time you have a Networking Meeting than you were the first one. and the fifth will be better than the third. Then anything can happen!

- Don't worry about meeting with the exact right person. meet with someone! Don't deliver the perfect message. deliver a message! The hardest part of any project is getting started. Always choose imperfect action over perfect inaction. There is no perfect action. just action that gets you closer to your next great career opportunity.

The interesting part of having guided hundreds of people through this process is that I cannot only predict how your job search will go, but I can forecast the mistakes that you will likely make. It's only human nature that people, given a highly-structured and predictable process, will try to circumvent it. These mistakes can most often be characterized as mistakes of ego. At the same time, these mistakes may be your best ally along the journey.

HSE can help you understand this whole ego-driven mistake factor. Remember, most people believe they can find their next position alone and without help. When I tell you that you need to be humble, be sincere, and ask for help, now remove your belief that asking for help is for weak people. As you can see through the *HSE* journey, the only thing weak about asking for help is not asking at all. It's a process, not a mind trip.

There you have it! Now go land through the *Human Search Engine* like hundreds of jobseekers already have in just a short period of time. You are part of a life-changing movement and an innovative launch of better connecting jobseekers to employers! Congratulations!

Chapter 27

A Plumber's Journey:
Your *Human Search Engine* model landing story.

This story best illustrates how this entire *Human Search Engine* process of definition, research, and marketing might work in the real world (and will work for you).

Imagine a plumber that moves to a new town and is looking to generate business for himself. He knows very few people in the town other than a few friends who are not in the plumbing industry.

His first effort is to create a wonderful marketing piece to randomly mail to all homeowners in town. In order to make sure that he doesn't "miss any opportunities" (sound familiar in your job search?), he makes this print piece as generic as possible. He indicates on his marketing piece that he can do "anything for anyone" and no job is too big or too small. He takes great pains to indicate every one of his areas of plumbing expertise on the brochure and assures people that he has the lowest prices in town with 24-hour-a-day service.

The plumber prints beautiful brochures (just like you do for your resumes) and distributes them to every house in town. Any home or apartment building that has plumbing is blanketed with his brochure. After distributing the brochures, he waits by the phone just knowing that soon it will be ringing off the hook.

Predictably, no one calls (how much do you respond to junk mail that is randomly sent to your house?). Our plumber is frustrated. He not only doesn't generate much interest, but he sees his brochures thrown out or recycled all over town (Does this sound familiar with your carefully worded resumes ending up in the "no pile?").

Out of frustration, our plumber decides to make himself available to people who need plumbing help by attending a home show. Clearly people at a home show are there for a reason and can likely be expected to have an interest in plumbing services. Just like you would promote yourself during a traditional job search, the plumber continues to do anything for anyone. New homes, old homes, geothermal heating systems, sink and toilet replacements. he can do it all. Surely now that he has cast a wide net over this group of people who have a similar interest in home building or remodeling (or they wouldn't have come to the home show), the plumber should now have people demanding his service.

The plumber does receive some calls after the show, but they are all for competitive pricing quotes. Subsequently, he only acquires a few of those jobs. Most often he finds that the jobs are going to more established plumbers in town who are being recommended to customers. The plumber is not being evaluated on his expertise or problem solving, but only on his pricing. Worse yet, because he has advertised that he can do any type of plumbing work, his prices are compared to EVERY type of plumber and handy man out there!

Out of sheer frustration, the plumber visits one of the few people in town who he knows and explains the problem to this person. This person asks the plumber, "What makes you unique enough for a stranger to want to hire you even when they have established existing plumbers to choose from?" The question at first oddly struck him; he hadn't really thought about it like that before. As the question became clearer to the plumber, it occurred to him that the people with plumbing jobs choose who to hire the same way that he has bought almost everything else. through a referral from someone known and trusted.

Given the opportunity to choose a stranger or someone who they know and trust, people will almost always go with what and who they know. People crave certainty, especially when talking about the biggest investment in their life. their house. The plumber's shoulders sagged as he started to think that there is no way a stranger can compete with existing plumbers in town.

A friend of the plumber asked him, "What do you specialize in?" He replied, "Well, I can do anything in the plumbing industry!" His friend furrows his brow and replies, "So you really don't have a specialty; you are just like every other plumber in town. No wonder people are evaluating you just on price. there is nothing unique about you."

After contemplating a bit, the plumber said, "Well, what I really do better than any plumber than I've ever met is replace corroded piping in old houses." "Now we're getting somewhere!" exclaims his friend. "Now we can start to get you in front of people who have the problems that you are uniquely able to solve."

The plumber's friend suggests that he completely redo all of his marketing materials to primarily focus on repairing piping on older houses. While afraid that he will be marketing to too narrow of an audience, he does realize that his "shotgun" approach didn't work. He spends some time defining a specific target audience for his message (**Definition phase**).

Next, the plumber's friend takes him and his newly targeted brochures to a meeting of the town's historical society. He thinks to himself, "What a waste of time. there are no plumbing jobs to be found there." While he sits in on the meeting, the plumber realizes that everyone there has a unique knowledge of the older, historic parts of the city, including the historic houses in the city. He also learns there is a community group that meets once a month that consists of people who own historic properties in the city. These people either own or deal directly with the owners of these properties. His friend introduces him to that group.

While fighting off the urge to ask if any of them needed work done on their homes or if they know of anyone who does, the plumber just asked questions of the group and learned everything he could about this historical properties group. In the course of this conversation, his friend (who is there to give him credibility as a good person and as a good plumber) suggests that he should be invited to the historical property group's next meeting as a guest.

At that meeting, the plumber begins to ask the property owners about what unique problems exist with owning and maintaining older buildings. He begins to understand their issues and problems, and he doesn't try to promote himself as a solution because that's not why he came to the meeting. The plumber came to gain knowledge from people who "live in the world he wants to live in". the world of historic home owners. He learns a great deal about specific problems they face, including trying to upgrade homes to today's codes, the struggle of replacing lead pipe with something that will not corrode, and the balance of updating while keeping the historical value of the house, etc. **(Research phase)**.

As the meeting continued, eventually someone asked the plumber specifically what he did for a living. Instead of saying, "I am a plumber who can fix any plumbing problem for anyone in any type of building," he simply provides a well-practiced statement: "I have been a plumber for more than 10 years, but really love to be involved with the refurbishing of the plumbing in older homes. Making these historic residences useable on a daily basis for people to live in really makes me happy." He smiles because this is no "sales line" to get their attention. it is a real explanation of his greatest joy in the world of plumbing.

The conversation quickly shifts to the plumber's experiences fixing the problems that the group had just laid out for him. He discusses his jobs related to historical houses in the town he just came from. He tells these stories with enthusiasm because doing this type of plumbing really does bring him joy.

The plumber is then asked by the group to present a portfolio of work photos. His work in older homes gives him credibility. His friend speaks up and says that he is a really great plumber because he has done work for him as well. The group of historic property owners now sees the plumber differently because he has credibility from his portfolio and third-party confirmation from someone who they already know as a person "who is who he says he is" **(Marketing phase)**.

Without much hesitation, one of the owners of the historic homes asked the plumber about a plumbing problem at her older home. At first she asked for advice, but eventually she asked him if he would be willing to come over and look at the problem (He couldn't push his way in; he had to be invited). The others say that if this job goes well, they would be happy to have him assess their properties as well.

Over the next month the plumber becomes the "go-to person" for the historic homeowners. People are calling him for his advice and guidance and making him the default choice for the work on their homes. Not only that, but historic homeowners start to refer this plumber to people who have much newer homes, but still need plumbing work.

People made their decision to hire the plumber based on the referrals of others, not on his price alone. How did he get here? Remember, a friend led him through the *HSE* process. No miracles, no accidents. it all makes so much sense now.

Chapter 28

Landings! Real People, Real Careers through *HSE*

Think differently. You are different

'I learned about my skills and how express them. A company learned of them too ... and hired me.' —Lisa B., 40

I had just earned my associate degree in Accounting and thought I'd explore whatever job search options were available. It was a brand new time for me as I was just entering the workforce after being a stay-at-home mom for several years. I met Chris Czarnik at an employment seminar at Fox Valley Technical College and was blown away at the experience.

I walked into that seminar thinking I didn't have much of a chance at ever landing a decent job. I really had no confidence in myself. As I watched him energetically present a clear plan on how to handle an interview, I began to think differently about searching for a job.

I then attended his job search sessions and learned the importance of setting goals and putting my achievements into words. This was something I didn't do well myself. Once I discovered how to effectively network my skills through Chris' guidance, I quickly realized what I had to offer to companies was an asset.

Although I had an office-related job working for a local automotive dealership— yes, in which I earned partly through Chris' guidance, I did not want to settle for doing something just to pass the time. I took the job at the time though to help my family financially. Once in that new position, however, I asked myself, "Why work just for sake of working?" It was then I put Chris' teachings into further action.

I set up a Networking Meeting with a past instructor and explained to her what I was looking for in a job. She recommended that I visit someone specific at a certain accounting firm. She thought I'd be a great fit there.

So, I hand-delivered my resume (which was requested—I did not leave this blindly), and a couple of days later the owner called me for a Networking Meeting. Notice how the arrangement was scheduled—as a 'networking meeting.' This is an important distinction from a formal interview.

After the meeting, the owner informed me that she didn't have any immediate openings. Not disappointed, I really left that meeting feeling better than after any interview I ever had; there was something special about it. I felt like I was important in her eyes and that the assessment of my credentials were not the only reason for the meeting.

About two months later the owner called and offered me a position! It was a position I had invested time and money toward, and here it was because of purposeful networking. So much for the kiss of death saying from hiring professionals, "We'll keep your name on file." That wasn't the case here! I was not treated like a "file." I had something the company needed as a unique "individual."

My growing confidence level during Chris' sessions played a big role in me landing this job. Success for me was not just about landing a great career; the whole process gave me a lifelong dose of invaluable advice. I now know how to better adapt in an ever-changing world.

I tell almost everyone how Chris can help them overcome fears and conquer any networking opportunity as a result of his new way to find a job. If you need a new direction in life, try Chris' approach. It brought success back into my life—in more ways than one.

You can't push your way into a job. I was pulled in.

'Many people believe the only way to network is with senior management. Not true! The keys to my career castle were handed to me by a C List contact.' —Dan S., 52

I was once in the groove of job security. With 30-plus years working in a mill in different capacities, ranging from laborer to training administrator, how could I not think this way? Then the day came in 2008 for about 600 of us; we received walking papers without any notice. After shaking off the shock, I realized I had two choices: sulk and feel sorry for myself and blame society or. get back in the game.

I have always believed in education. I realized I could use some government funding for retraining with a little of my savings to invest in some education. I enrolled in the Applied Engineering Technology program at Fox Valley Technical College, and I was proudly on pace to graduate with an associate degree in about two years. It was fun, challenging, and very rewarding. I even saw some of my former co-workers from the mill attending various classes around the college!

So, here I was in my early 50s pursuing a degree, but in need of a job. I have also done enough baseline job search exploration to realize I was stuck in the quandary of competing against younger talent for the next job. That said, I was very intrigued on how to land my first job in more than three decades. I wasn't thrilled about hitting the classified ads. So I heard about Chris Czarnik's job search sessions and starting attending them with an open mind.

My open mind widened during his first session, not by choice. He installed an immediate sense of humility in me and others. He did so by saying no one knows you exist and no one is going to hold your hand and sing "Kumbaya." Wow--what a harsh, yet inspirational greeting. That first meeting alone made me zero in on what this person had up his sleeve for us.

After attending a few sessions, I started to get it. Chris' methodology was unlike anything I had ever heard of before concerning how to find a job. This is not to mention a "job" that you like. Without this resource, I am convinced I would not be working today as a safety manager for a large, local pulp and paper company.

Looking back, it's Chris' ABC List that gave me the keys to this career castle in 2011. If it wasn't for his wake up call that networking is not 'networking' unless it is orchestrated and relevant, I would not be enjoying this great job, which originated as a safety engineer position. The ABC List was the catalyst for making my networking successful.

The C List in particular was a gold mine for me. A former mill co-worker of mine, Jeff, landed a job earlier in the year for the same company. He did so through Chris' sessions too. He was one of the individuals on my C List when I went through Chris' sessions. Jeff suggested that I talk to some middle management people at the company, who became new B List contacts for me. I did so, and these individuals referred me personally to A List people at the company.

In each case along this process, Jeff and the B List people paved the way for me to the A List contacts. I learned early in Chris' class that no one can "push his or her way into a job." Ambushing one's way into the busy lives of senior-level managers is both a turn off and a mutual waste of time.

A couple of A List folks agreed to meet with me (separately) to have an Informal Interview about my goals and experiences. During these conversations I never asked them for a job, but I planted seeds about my skills. At the end of my second meeting, I asked for some potential referrals (all part of building a network during the *HSE* process). The response was, "Why not work here?"

The individual told me about the company's safety needs and believe I could solve their problems! My job was literally created for me. They needed me and built a position for me. Since my hiring as a safety engineer in 2011, I have been promoted to safety manager. What Chris is teaching really works.

I Thought I Knew Everything About Searching for a Job. Ouch.

'Somewhere along the way in applying to nearly 400 jobs and going through 30-plus interviews, I failed to find a job. Jobseekers need to understand that times have changed.' —Ron S., 55

I lived through a two-year stint of unemployment, and I'd like to address the age factor first as a reason (or not a reason) for being unable to find a job. I know many people think HR reps discriminate against older candidates. That claim is true because I heard it to my face. Subsequently, I had to rethink my disposition for a moment as it relates to career search.

What I realized were two things: First, I wouldn't want to work for someone anyway that viewed people in the context of age. Second, I could have complained about my experience as being told I was over the hill and held grudges, but what would that accomplish? I then discovered, and you will too, that the *Human Search Engine* removes virtually all stereotypical discriminatory actions anyway. Why? Its process is predicated on connecting genuine professionals to solve mutual problems—that's it.

My primary field of Information Technology (IT) was not to blame either for me not earning employment. My lack of success was also not due to being out of work for too long or lack of experience or skills (I have a 90-page professional portfolio). The bottom line. the failure was in my approach to finding a job.

Finding a rewarding job today has nothing to do with numbers of applicants, someone's age, or the size of a portfolio, to name a few reasons. In cases where these traits do openly or perceptually play a role in job search, I have learned they are irrelevant if you do your job search the right way.

The wrong way to conduct a job search is to do what I first did. I scoured the Internet, newspaper listings, and billboards to apply for every job I thought I fit the description for or that I could do. Through this process, the furthest I ever advanced in landing a job in two years was three, second-round interviews. Notice I mentioned the word "process" in the previous sentence. One lesson I learned for sure from traditional career search is that combing through every medium for job ads is not a process.

Don't be fooled by thinking that doing all the functions of a traditional job search method constitutes a process. I know this method can still land people jobs. I also know that more of today's employers are learning that staying competitive in a global market means their hiring practices require a new strategy. Therefore, I discovered there is a mismatch when it comes to conventional job search methods and how companies are looking to find the right people. The result is failure—not just for the job hunter, but also for any business.

HSE is a true process, and it originally landed me an incredible job making six figures as a solution architect for an IT firm through organized, strategic networking that was devised by applying instructional steps. I earned this position in a less than a quarter of the time it took me to endure all those other failing job search attempts. Furthermore, I was making more money than ever doing what I loved to do.

Sadly, after 13 months that position was abruptly eliminated in early 2012. Once again, my layoff was another reminder of how competitive and unstable the job market is today. We can't predict the decisions companies make, but we can manage our reactions and next moves related to being unemployed. After receiving the bad news, I instantly turned to *HSE* again. In less than three weeks, this process produced seven new connections that led to three job offers!

These new connections morphed into career options for me. Yes, I had options in an economy where we hear there are no jobs. I had offers to consider without posting a single resume to help me rebound from my recent layoff. One of those offers developed in a way that made me realize the power of *HSE*.

I was preparing for a second interview with an insurance company and discovered ahead of time that the interviewer also went through *HSE* (Czar told me about this person during a conversation in which his name came up). I was also informed prior to the interview from the insurance company that it would last about an hour. During the first minute of the interview I mentioned Czar's program to the hiring manager. He paused and replied, "Ron, this interview is over. I am such an advocate of *Human Search Engine* that any 'graduate' of that program is top notch in my book."

The manager concluded, "We've already determined that you have the technical skills for the job from the first interview. The second interview was to get to know you and determine if you could fit into our mix of staff. I'm convinced that anyone who goes through *HSE* will provide the drive and leadership we're looking for." The interview was over in about 10 minutes. Within a week the company offered me a position.

The same day I was about to accept the position with the insurance company, this whole *HSE* thing unimaginably materialized some more. I had just received another offer, and this job was from one of the largest consulting companies in the world. I recalled recently making contact with this company through my "A List" during *HSE*. The personnel manager I spoke with on the phone who offered me the job said that the company couldn't let me get away.

Not that money is everything and I certainly know that from experience, but the consulting company's salary package exceeded the one that was currently on the table from the insurance company by 144%. Consequently, I accepted the newer offer as a technology manager with the consulting firm. I then contacted the insurance firm and another company that had an outstanding offer in my lap to thank them both for their respective opportunities.

My *HSE* journey was incredible because of not only the job prospects, but because I learned a process that really works if you follow the steps. I didn't think there were a whole lot of positive employment stories left in a world full of constant doom and gloom as projected by negative media. Aside from my unusual and dually-successful chronicle of landing a job, here's what I want to share with others about *HSE*:

Think of *HSE* as a "career of choice" plan. If you do the work, you'll be successful. "Work" in this sense conceptually blows away the wasted energy and exhausting grind of a traditional job search. The work put into *HSE* is measurable every step of the way, and it is a lifelong skill that I may use someday in other professional and personal contexts.

First, right from Czar's mouth, erase your mind from everything "you thought you knew about landing a job."

- Shut up and listen. I don't intend to sound blunt, but so many people want to interject all the time during a job search session or workshop. I convinced myself to listen instead of interjecting. Then I started to believe in the *HSE* process.

- Do the work that Czar outlines. *HSE* is not a "social activity" that will land you a job. Just work on the exercises as a step-by-step process and you will be rewarded.

Admittedly, I was skeptical about *HSE* at first. Looking back after doing the work, I now wish that employers and jobseekers can better align their synergies if they knew more about *HSE*. By doing so, the result would add tremendous value to our quality of life, our economy, and our workforce.

My rewarding career is not solely based on salary, benefits, or anything of that nature. I am elated because *HSE* gave me a chance to prove that "old dogs are not dead," and we can prosper with the best of them in any industry. Regardless of one's age, maybe I will read or hear more successes about *HSE* as time rolls on. this is something that should not be "a best kept secret."

Career Planners and Job Fairs: Why was I Still Unemployed?

'In one year, I attended every job search event around and worked with a career planning firm. Then after attending one HSE session, I discovered an extraordinary process that led to a job and a life skill.' —Jamie V., 41

Like most jobseekers in today's economy, I tried to find worthwhile employment on my own. I had no success. I left a job of 14 years to better myself with a new employer, where after nine months, that job was eliminated. There I was in my late 30s without a job. My husband was working, so I could dive into the world of job searching, career planning consultation, and thanks to the Web, saturate my credentials to countless employers. No problem. I was ready to use all of these tactics to find another job, anchored by my nearly of 25 years of professional work experience.

I soon realized all career programs and job search events are basically the same, and 90% of the time organizations didn't even acknowledge my applications. My job-search appeared to be rather impersonal and unplanned. I was getting all kinds of talk, but no action. I don't know why it took me so long to realize that this path to employment was not working.

Then I heard about a job search class at Fox Valley Technical College. It appeared intriguing enough to check out. My story is likely a bit different from even other *HSE* participants. The majority of those who continue to land jobs from Czar's process do so in less than three months if they do the work. Infamously, and to no fault of Czar, it took me about three years to land a job.

Here's why. At one of the early *HSE* sessions, I discovered that the actual process to finding a fulfilling career could also apply to so many other aspects of life—like researching leisure activities, a project, and so on. I was so enthralled at this process that I wrote everything down like it was the lecture of a lifetime. I asked myself, "Where in the heck has this service been?" Perhaps that question was as equally as fascinating as the simplicity and significance of the *HSE* process. Ironically, that question has been answered in this book.

Again, I probably overindulged myself in every competency taught by Czar in his sessions. For me, it was a big picture look at a life skill, not to mention of course—a manageable process full of usable tactics in landing a job. I had to occasionally remind myself that I was there because I needed to find a job. I started answering Czar's questions before he would ask them.

Through my initial experiences attending his sessions and absorbing the material, I was asked by Czar's department at the college to manage its database.

I was ecstatic and an instant supporter in what Czar was teaching! His sessions opened a door for me in the department to learn more about hiring in general, including what jobs area companies had available, their strong connections to technical colleges, and more. The position also allowed me to stay connected to Czar's job search sessions.

This part-time job (and I never applied for it through Monster.com or any other Web or conventional job posting like a newspaper or a broadcast ad) led to teaching classes on LinkedIn and on job search strategies for current students. In addition to my new roles, albeit part-time, I continued to volunteer around the community. What a great move, personally and professionally! I recall Czar mentioning the importance of volunteering during *HSE*. Think about it. While giving to others, you can make connections and prepare for working in diverse workplaces on your next job.

During all of these experiences, I had neglected my own *HSE* personal job search to help others find work. I was, however, making all kinds of professional connections at networking events, and soon I would realize how to make the most of these relationships. The only shortcoming about my job at the college and the volunteer positions was that my husband and I were on the verge of depleting our savings.

I ended up working over two years on my part-time job at the college. I needed to refocus my attention on *HSE*. The primary emphasis for me at this point in the process was digging deeply into my C List of contacts. It's important to remember you can't just "network" into a job without some strategy.

You have to make people *like you*. If a door is opened through a referral, you still have to make the interaction relevant and positive. The winning formula is based on conveying the right credentials with a professional attitude—both attributes that the *HSE* process refines to near perfection for you if you do the work.

My C List had grown due to what I learned through *HSE*, including who to network with, how to create networking scenarios, and what to say when those opportunities surfaced. These experiences increased my confidence. Long story, short. I networked my way to an interview for a local health care organization.

The interview landed me a full-time job, where I coordinate contracts, invoices, site visits, and events. I work with organizations across the United States and Canada. I love it! I learned after I was hired that I made the best first impression of all the candidates. My supervisor said I exuded energy and passion while discussing my skills, making me the best "fit" for the job. That goes to show you the power of *HSE*. The process had prepared me for this moment—it enabled me to first attain the interview and then hammer it home successfully.

The reality is. finding a job today depends on as much as being part of the "right mix" as it does having the skills to do the job. Your personality, professionalism, and ability to fit into a workplace culture are bigger factors than ever before in today's hiring process. Fair or unfair, it's the playing field.

Your coach for this 21st Century game with the know-how to land wins (a job is a "win" in the correlation) for his players is the Czar, and his team is *HSE*. It changed my life and set my future on the right track. Thankfully, *HSE* is being offered for the betterment of our society!

Chapter 29

Employers: Welcome to Smart Hiring

Smart companies don't make half-a-million-dollar decisions off of a piece of paper

Jobseekers have no more idea where to look for a position that fits them than the organizations do on where to find their next great employee. It's that simple. Yet closing this disconnect has been very complex. until now. Let's explore this disconnect a bit more with employers in mind this time.

Today, a jobseeker can post a resume to the Web and throw his or her credentials across the world in the snap of two fingers. An employer can also post a job and instantly present it to millions of people. This appears to be a far cry from a disconnect. what's wrong with saturating the universe to find the best of the best?

Armed with speed, flare, and instantaneous multiple audiences, the Web, broadcast media, and traditional newspapers (including their online editions), and even recruitment firms, are disproportionate in three critical areas when it comes to finding talent: cost, time, and quality. Remember. once upon a time when jobs were everywhere and the world was less populated, less complex, not as globally connected, and less politically charged, the labor force had room for faceless figures to fill a plethora of positions. That reality is now just a page in a history book.

Before examining **cost, time,** and **quality** in greater detail, it is imperative to understand that they have clearer ramifications to the way business is done today. Manufacturing and health care, for instance, have adopted LEAN principles more than ever to stay afloat by cutting costs and waste. Look at data from any community college across the United States and learn that its graduates possess skills that companies are actually crying for. quality is defined in this context as having a hands-on skill and credibility. This level of education is outdoing bachelor's degrees in terms of importance today. Times have changed. We either accept this reality and adapt or spend our time arguing and drifting away (just like traditional job search methods).

Cost

One of the reasons I enjoy working in education, primarily at the community college level, is that success is measurable. Graduate placement is measured annually and job data is updated daily, to provide just a few examples. There isn't a whole lot of theory-based babble going on with this brand of education. it's about straight talk and hands-on learning.

When pursuing your next career or anything in life that matters, progress ought to be measurable as well. The issue most jobseekers have is that they are trying to measure success within a failing system—and that alone is a challenge! The *HSE* process demands from its learners a commitment to measuring points of achievement along the way through assessing Return-On-Investment, or ROI.

Let's think about ROI in the simplest of terms to help frame why 'smart hiring' with *HSE* is amazingly cost-effective. When you go out to eat and buy dinner, the ROI is that you are no longer hungry. When you invest to fix your roof, the ROI is that there will be no leaks and your home will have a greater resale value. When you make a donation to a charity, the ROI is that you helped a non-profit organization buy door prizes for its annual fundraiser.

For companies looking to fill open positions, advertising in newspapers, on broadcast networks, and on Web sites through resources like Monster, Career Builder, and The Ladders, etc., costs a lot of money. What's the ROI? The honest answer for any company using these methods of hiring is nothing more than a **shot in the dark.** I'm sure there aren't many ROIs that businesses are willing to pursue through a **shot in the dark.** The problem is these methods are all they've known for a long time.

Let's briefly examine the ballpark cost of hiring one employee by using three common mediums similar to the ones mentioned in the previous paragraph. We'll do so by using a simple comparison chart below that illustrates TRADITIONAL vs. *HSE* hiring practices:

Cost of Hiring One Employee: TRADITIONAL Method:

(Based on posting a job for 2 weeks through newspaper, Web, and broadcast media):

- Two Sunday ads in the local newspaper (includes Web): $750
- One posting via a traditional online resource, like mentioned above (based on the average costs of the three above): $450 (Note: This method comes with an option to pay, on average, another $600 to be able to review online resumes for a 30-day minimum. For sake of our calculation, we'll conservatively say half of the companies in this example opt for the service, so we can add another $300)

- An ad purchase on a medium-size market radio station to air over two weeks: $1,500
- TOTAL AVERAGE COST: $3,000
- Question: HAVE YOU FOUND THE BEST TALENT IN JUST TWO WEEKS?
- Lastly, this method doesn't account for human resources costs associated with the screening of applicants, interviews, and reference checks. More on these factors later in this chapter.

Cost of Hiring One Employee: *HSE* Method:
(Based on nothing except maybe a phone call, an email, or a cup of coffee)

FREE. No catches, no bells, no whistles. it is completely free to hire any number of employees at any time through *HSE*.

Why is smart hiring through *HSE* free? It doesn't require the posting of any jobs. It is based on employers informing the *HSE* network on what talent is needed, and the process does the rest by matching qualified people with the needs of companies. That's it!

As you can see, the upfront costs of placing job posting ads for one employee can run at least $2,000–$3,000, and that's just using a few different mediums like those mentioned above as examples. Then an employer has to consider how long to run the ads if qualified candidates aren't responding to them, and that contributes to additional costs.

It makes me wonder how many **shots in the dark** would still be part of the hiring game if more employers were 'smart companies' in partnership with *HSE*. Yes, *HSE* would have to be offered across the country for this to make a dent; hence the reason why the word needs to get out!

Time

'Smart hiring' the *HSE* way not only influences an employer's bottom line, but it is as simple as placing an order through a drive-through restaurant. Whether your company needs an IT professional, a market research assistant, a sales manager, or anyone in between, it just needs to "place an order" with *HSE*. Then through a fluid, growing network of professionals, the process yields talent from its pool of A-B-C Lists, class sessions, or *HSE* "alumni." As *HSE* grows, so does its network.

Companies strive on saving time and money. LEAN principles directly correlate to both of these workplace success factors. The *HSE* process plays right into LEAN organizations—again, the growing buzz concept behind today's businesses.

HSE saves companies time in the following areas as a comparison to conventional human resource hiring practices:

- No need to post advertised job announcements (broadcast, Web, newspaper, etc.) – Note: Companies can still post job announcements on their own Websites.
- No need to process and review resumes
- No need to schedule and conduct formal interviews – Note: Remember, through *HSE* Informational Interviews take place, but these are done mostly in neutral, non-threatening settings with more subtle expectations (over a cup of coffee or lunch, at a community function, etc.)
- No need to conduct formal references

Think of all the employee development initiatives that HR professionals can exert their energy on to increase retention when removing these procedural hiring barriers. Employee retention is a whole other area of 21st Century workplace prioritization that is only briefly touched on in this book (next paragraph). Do you see the impact of *HSE* beyond its immediate benefits of addressing the job search and hiring dilemma?

Quality (of talent)

We've established *HSE*'s impact on both time and money for businesses. Now, let's glance inside perhaps the biggest challenge facing today's employers: finding the right people to fill the right jobs. The saturation of job announcements through multi-media channels is attracting maybe a solid match every once in a while, and yes, people are trainable. That said, I may win the lottery tomorrow.

Remember our friend from earlier in this chapter, "**shot in the dark**"? Thankfully, we don't do everything in life as a **shot in the dark**. Imagine the condition of our roads, mortality rates at nursing homes, the cleanliness of the food we eat, and so on. if everything was done as a **shot in the dark**. Building roads, administering medicine, and growing crops are all done in a calculated manner. Why should hiring your next employee be any different?

Until *HSE* catches on, finding the right talent for companies continues to be a roll of dice. Businesses invest a "half-a-million-dollar decision" each day off of a piece of paper and off of interviews based on little or no prior connection. On the other hand, hiring employees through *HSE* is quite a logical move:

ced *HSE* jobseekers are pre-qualified professionals because of the process they have undergone:

- Since the *HSE* process is *logical*, jobseekers learn how to manage their own job search plan with a high level of accountability. Everything they do during the process makes sense. It is a like taking a class where the competencies can be immediately applied. It is a plan that is being followed by hundreds of people who are landing jobs by following a process. Do the work and you will be rewarded.

- Since the *HSE* process is *sequential*, jobseekers have demonstrated patience and commitment to something outside of their comfort level. In other words, *HSE* jobseekers are responsible because they have remained true to a step-by-step process. Ironically, in a recent survey conducted by New North (a regional economic development organization representing 18 counties in northeast Wisconsin), **83% of businesses indicated they look for responsibility as the number one trait of an employee.**
- Since the *HSE* process is *experiential*, jobseekers have engaged in numerous activities about themselves and have communicated with several diverse individuals as part of their networking experience. *HSE* jobseekers will live through failure, adaptation, self-revelation, and success during the process.
- Since the *HSE* process is terminal, jobseekers land jobs. The time it takes each jobseeker to reach this objective is different for everyone. In addition, it's important to remember that *HSE* jobseekers land jobs they actually like too!

The bottom line is that *HSE* is a culture, a network, and a process that people can relate to because of its symmetry and affiliation to results. Participants are navigating in the same boat, they speak the same job search lingo, and all of them understand the real purpose of networking. When a referral is made in connection to *HSE*, that word is as good as gold.

Michael Johnson is an HR professional with 15 years of experience in hiring talent. He would know about the benefits of *HSE* first-hand because he's used it from both sides of the aisle. Johnson experienced the process first as a jobseeker after learning about it from his wife, who attended a session in-between classes while going to college. She urged Michael to also attend after proclaiming to him excitedly, "He's teaching career search as a process and as a skill!"

"There I was, humiliated and embarrassed to be at *HSE* because I was unemployed and thought I already knew how to find a job," says Johnson. "Up to this moment, I had been relatively successful in interviewing and finding new employment on my own schedule. This time around I was going nowhere with an unsuccessful job search using the Internet and job posting sites."

Johnson sought employment in this manner for about six weeks before attending his first *HSE* session. "Every day, seemingly all day, I would submit posting after posting because I thought this was the only way to find a job in the current business world," he adds. "I was embarrassed to admit that I needed help finding a job because I simply no longer knew how to do it without answering an ad."

After being humbled, Johnson declared that he followed the steps outlined in *HSE*, did the work, and found success in his current career that is now approaching two years. He certainly represents a 'smart company' in my region that is catching the *HSE* wave.

In his current role as manager of application development for a national insurance company, Johnson continues to work directly in the process of hiring, developing, and retaining talent. His exposure to several hiring methods over the years only reaffirms that none of them bridge the ongoing disconnect between jobseekers and employers.

"Over the years I've been hiring corporate employees for many positions using methods like targeted selection, behavioral predictors, The Interview Architect®, and panel interviews," says Johnson. "When you peel back the layers of these hiring methods and most others, they're all basically the same. The *Human Search Engine* was the first technique I ever encountered that seamlessly links pre-screened talent to companies for free!"

For Johnson's company, hiring the *HSE* way is not only cost effective and efficient, but the process involves a personal recommendation from other *HSE* members or from me. He continues, "A 'personal recommendation' means that the candidate is thought of in such high standing, and he or she comes with genuine credibility. Think about it. the recommending party is putting a lot at stake here. The whole process is that trustworthy."

Cost and quality are inarguably both saving graces for companies and their human resource practices today, according to Johnson. "*HSE* does not involve expensive job postings or recruiters and fees," he notes. "It does include hundreds of current and past members who are actively either looking for the right job or seeking to help others find their next career."

Johnson continues to use *HSE* in two ways. First, he subscribes to the job search group on LinkedIn. Here he has an instant connection to currently more than 500 members to advertise positions that his company is hiring for, and he contributes regularly to the discussions.

Second, Johnson uses LinkedIn to make connections with jobseekers. He often meets them for lunch or coffee to share his *HSE* story too. "It's the least I can do and I enjoy it," he notes. "I encourage them to continue networking the right way and perfecting their 60-Second Introduction."

He's right. *HSE* does not use a job board, have any postings, or an application process. It teaches the fundamentals of how to talk to people and give them relevant information to help you find the right job. It's that simple, and now you've heard it from an employer's voice. The longtime mismatch between jobseekers and employers is definitely a deterrent to any economy—imagine the potential if more people and more companies saw career search differently.

Inquiries~

For more information about what Career Research Group can do for you or your organization, or to book Chris as a guest speaker you can find us at:

        www.careerresearchgroup.com
        Or email us at:
        info@careerresearchgroup.com

About The Authors~

Chris Czarnik

Chris is a career search advisor with 11 years of job search counseling experience and motivational speaking, in addition to 15 years of experience working as a manager in the manufacturing sector. He has presented job search strategy in front of hundreds of people, in addition to providing classroom and one-on-one consultation. His work has helped more than a thousand jobseekers land rewarding careers.

Chris currently serves as a career search counselor for Wisconsin's largest two-year college (based on total number of people served), Fox Valley Technical College, and is a leading adjunct career search instructor for the 5th largest research university in the nation, the University of Wisconsin-Madison. He also wrote the career search curriculum for the university's athletic department. Both the University of Wisconsin Colleges and the Wisconsin Technical College System have utilized Chris' expertise as a career search speaker. Most recently, Chris was a featured speaker at the 2013 National Career Search Conference in Madison.

Christopher Jossart, M.A.

Chris is a public relations management professional with 20 years of experience in the non-profit, for-profit, and education fields. He currently serves as manager of media relations for Fox Valley Technical College, the largest two-year college in Wisconsin (based on total number of people served), and has been serving as a college communications instructor for the past 11 years.

Chris is a published author with international and national bylines, mostly in the areas of education, training, and community development. He also serves as the executive editor of an award-winning national higher education magazine, with an annual direct distribution of nearly 100,000 readers. In addition, Chris has presented at national conferences on topics related to volunteer development and retention, and his written several recognition-related nominations that have earned awards for volunteers of all ages. Those nominations have been used as a model for non-profit organizations in the areas of volunteer development.

Sample Networking Brief

JOHN SMITH, CPA, MBA

1313 MOCKINGBIRD LANE, APPLETON, WI 54915
PHONE: (920) 555-1212 • E-MAIL: johnsmith@yahoo.com
URL: www.linkedin.com/in/johnsmith

Search Objective:
Chief Financial Officer or Controller position in a small to medium company to manage the accounting function to provide accurate, complete, and timely financial data with comprehensive analysis necessary for making sound business decisions and achieving performance goals.

Background and experience:
5 years – Senior Vice President & Chief Financial Officer – Choice Bank
10+ years – Vice President Finance (CFO) – Oshkosh Savings Bank
8+ years teaching college level accounting, finance, and general business

Skill set:

Bachelor of Science, Accounting	Masters of Business Administration
Certified Public Accountant (CPA)	SEC reporting
Start-up bank	Financial analysis
Budgeting and long-range planning	Capital campaigns
Bank regulatory reporting	Manage accounting team
Freelance writer	Teach accounting to non-accountants

Achievements:
Experienced Chief Financial Officer (CFO). Accounting and analytical skills readily transferable to any industry. "Hands-on" leader. Prepared three-year financial business plan to earn charter for start-up bank in Oshkosh. Did all record-keeping and provided assistance for shareholders in start-up bank to raise a Wisconsin record of $21.6 million in capital and start bank that has grown. Served as CFO to help bank grow to $120 million in assets in three years and achieve profitability in third year. Did all Securities & Exchange Commission (SEC) and bank regulatory reporting for start-up bank.

Companies of interest:
Kimberly Clark
PepsiCo
BMO Harris
General Electric
Boeing
Hewlett-Packard Company
Microsoft
Chase
AIG

Sample Informational Interview Request Letter/Email

John Smith, CPA, MBA
1313 Mockingbird Lane, Appleton, WI 54915
Phone (920) 555-1212.   E-MAIL johnsmith@yahoo.com
URL:www.linkedin.com/in/johnsmith

April 24, 2012

Mr. Rick Simons
Director of Finance
First National Bank and Trust
Milwaukee, WI 53203

Dear Mr. Simons:

Tina Wilson suggested I contact you because of your expertise in the area of banking and finance systems. I am on a career search and would value your insight and experience in the field of banking in the Milwaukee area.

Please understand that I do not expect you to have or know of opportunities at this time. I am going about my career search in a way that I believe will produce better results than conventional methods.

I have been involved in all aspects of finance for the last seven (7) years, but my passion is in the direction of large real estate transactions where I utilize my leadership, analytical and problem solving abilities. The leadership and solutions I bring to a team make a difference in the implementation of lean banking initiatives. This work has increased the organization's level of internal quality systems and improved the loan approval process while reducing their overall costs. I want to continue in this direction and pursue a position in the banking and finance sector in the greater Milwaukee area.

I would like a brief meeting with you to discuss banking and the need for lean practices in a finance setting. I will also be asking for some advice and feedback.

I will call you on Wednesday, April 30th mid-morning, to set a convenient time to meet. I will come prepared and very much look forward to meeting you. I understand you are busy, and promise to be brief.

Sincerely,

John Smith

Acknowledgements

1. (**page 6**) – Fox Valley Technical College's Student Employment Services department in Appleton, Wisconsin is the owner of the JobSeekers Network (JSN) model.

2. (**page 8**) – Data from Wisconsin TechConnect, an online employment information system for recruiting Wisconsin Technical College System students and graduates for all types of employment (June 2012).

3. (**page 15**) – Dependable Strengths Articulation Process created by Drs. Bernard and Jean Haldane (1945), Bernard Haldane & Associates. Center for Dependable Strengths (CDS), Seattle, Washington (2002).

4. (**page 16**) - Email exchange provided as messaging content from one of the recipients, Christopher Czarnik (1984). Names used in *Human Search Engine* as part of this email correspondence are fictitious.

5. (**page 17**) – www.consumeraffairs.com, summary of legal activity regarding Bernard Haldane & Associates between 2003 and 2010, and www.ripoffreport.com, summarizes hundreds of consumer complaints between 2002 and 2011 concerning Bernard Haldane & Associates

6. (**page 20**) – "50/50" Club a name referred with Fox Valley Technical College's JobSeekers Network (JSN)

7. (**page 37**) – www.myersbriggs.org

8. (**page 37**) – www.myersbriggs.org

Photographs of authors taken by Coalesce Marketing and Design and Adam Shea Photography